A Right Royal History

Terrance Dicks
Illustrated by Kathryn Lamb

A RIGHT ROYAL HISTORY
A THOUSAND YEARS OF MIXED-UP
MONARCHY

TERRANCE DICKS
ILLUSTRATED BY KATHRYN LAMB

PICCADILLY PRESS • LONDON

Text copyright © Terrance Dicks, 1994
Illustration copyright © Kathryn Lamb, 1994

First published 1994
Reprinted 1994

Typeset from author's disc by James Kelly
Printed and bound by Biddles Ltd., Guildford, Surrey
for the publishers
Piccadilly Press Ltd., 5 Castle Road, London NW1 8PR

ISBNs: 1 85340 248 6 (hardback), 1 85340 253 2 (trade paperback)

Terrance Dicks lives in North London. A very well known author he has written numerous books. Among his popular information humour books published by Piccadilly Press, he has written: *A Riot of Writers*, *A Riot of Irish Writers*, *Europe United* and, most recently, *Uproar in the House*.

Kathryn Lamb lives in Dorset. She has illustrated many humour and children's books, often working in collaboration with her husband Adrian Bovey - while she draws the illustrations, he colours them. She also illustrated *Staying Cool, Surviving School* for Piccadilly Press.

CONTENTS

A RIGHT ROYAL FAMILY TREE

THE NORMANS

WILLIAM I 1066 - 1087
WILLIAM II 1087 - 1100
HENRY I 1100 - 1135
STEPHEN 1135 - 1154

THE HOUSE OF TUDOR

HENRY VII 1485 - 1509
HENRY VIII 1509 - 1547
EDWARD VI 1547 - 1553
MARY I 1553 - 1558
ELIZABETH I 1558 - 1603

THE STUARTS

JAMES I 1603 - 1625
CHARLES I 1625 - 1649
CHARLES II 1660 - 1685
JAMES II 1685 - 1688
WILLIAM III 1689 - 1702
AND
MARY II 1689 - 1694
ANNE 1702 - 1714

THE HOUSE OF HANOVER

GEORGE I 1714 - 1727
GEORGE II 1727 - 1760
GEORGE III 1760 - 1820
GEORGE IV 1820 - 1830
WILLIAM IV 1830 - 1837

ALFRED THE GREAT 871 - 899
EDWARD THE CONFESSOR 1042 - 1066
HAROLD II 1066

THE EARLY PLANTAGENETS

HENRY II 1154 - 1189
RICHARD I 1199 - 1199
JOHN 1199 - 1216
HENRY III 1216 - 1272
EDWARD I 1272 - 1307
EDWARD II 1307 - 1327
EDWARD III 1327 - 1377
RICHARD II 1377 - 1399

THE PLANTAGENETS

HENRY IV 1399 - 1413
HENRY V 1413 - 1422
HENRY VI 1422 - 1471
EDWARD IV 1461 - 1483
RICHARD III 1483 - 1485

1837 - 1901
VICTORIA

THE HOUSE OF WINDSOR

VICTORIA 1837 - 1901
EDWARD VII 1901 - 1910
GEORGE V 1910 - 1936
EDWARD VIII 1936
GEORGE VI 1936 - 1952
ELIZABETH II 1952 —

VIC LUVS ALBERT
QUEENVIC WOZ ERE
SO WOZ EDWARD VII
GEORGE V WOZ ERE
AND GEORGE VI WOZ
E.R. (H.R.H.) RULES O.K.

INTRODUCTION

A Right Royal Scandal

Some of today's Royals seem to be always in trouble.

Not Her ever-so-gracious Majesty herself - and not of course, our lovable old Queen Mum.

Even Prince Philip - Phil the Greek, as *Private Eye* so unkindly calls him - seems pretty free of scandal these days, barring the odd tactless remark.

(On a trip to China he's said to have told an English student, 'Don't stay out here too long, you'll get slitty eyes.')

But the rest of them...

Prince Charles falling off horses and talking to tulips.

Lady Di doing her new Greta Garbo act. ('I want to be alone!')

The Camilla tapes, the Squidgy tapes, high-living Princess Margaret and high-horsey Princess Anne, Randy Andy and his topless Duchess, the theatrical Edward...

Royal Soap

Sometimes our royal soap opera seems enough to keep the tabloid press busy all by itself.

Like a recent bishop, you might feel like saying, 'Shocking!'

But if you know a bit of history, you're more likely to say, 'So what?'

The truth is, our royals have always been pretty hot stuff.

Respectable royalty arrived with Queen Victoria. Before that - well, the tabloid press would have had a ball. (If there'd been any tabloid press. In those days discussing royal secrets could earn you a long stay in the Tower of London - or a short sharp shock from the executioner's axe.)

Back to Basics

Let's get back to royal basics, and take a closer look at those so-called good old days.

When a king dies, it's immediately a matter of:
The king is dead, long live the king!'

THIS CROWN WAS
DESIGNED TO PROTECT
THE KING FROM AN ATTACK
FROM ABOVE

CROWNS WERE
SOMETIMES ATTRACTIVE
TO NESTING BIRDS

SPECIAL 'HAPPY BIRTHDAY
YOUR MAJESTY!' CROWN

WET WEATHER CROWN

INTRODUCTION

His majesty pops the royal clogs and the eldest son steps, or rather sits, smartly on the throne. Though don't forget, some of our best kings have been queens - Victoria for one, and the respective Elizabeths for two!

In early times, being king was more like being the boss of a big corporation - or heavyweight champion of the world.

You got the job if you were tough enough to grab it, and kept it only as long as you could hold on to it.

Family Values

There were always plenty of rivals, usually amongst your nearest and dearest. (Knocking off any ambitious male relatives was considered a wise career move by most early monarchs.)

One of any monarch's main concerns was to provide a son and heir to take over when the time came. If there was no clear candidate, the job was up for grabs again - which could mean a long and bloody civil war.

THE FIRST PUB

The Romans Arrive

Like everywhere else England was finally invaded by the all-conquering Roman Empire. It took the roaming Romans twenty years to take over. The last real rebel was Boadicea, the lady with the knife-blades on her chariot. She was finally defeated in AD 62. The Romans never did manage to conquer the savage Scots, so they settled for building Hadrian's Wall to keep them out.

Romans Go Home!

The Romans ruled England and Wales for over three hundred years. They eventually had to go home when their empire was over-run by hoards of hairy barbarians. (Maybe the over-civilised Romans spent too much time shaving.)

When they finally left, early in the fifth century, everything fell into disorder and confusion. England was attacked by Angles, Saxons and Jutes from Germany, and later by the first tourists, the invading Vikings. The invaders were fought off by a variety of local warlords, some of whom started calling themselves kings. Our early kings were really regional rulers, and as well as fighting invaders they often attacked each other.

There were seven warring English kingdoms in Saxon times, with Northumbria, Mercia and Wessex amongst the most powerful. Wessex eventually emerged as top kingdom. Ecgberht of Wessex - these early kings had very weird names - reigned from 802 to 839, and has a good claim to be called the first English king.

ALFRED THE GREAT - 871-899

Most memorable of these early monarchs was Alfred the Great, who spent his reign trying to discourage those Danish invaders. (The Danes treated England like a Saturday-morning supermarket, popping over regularly for a quick bit of looting and pillaging. Some of them liked it so much they decided to stay. They formed colonies in England, and there were even some Danish kings.)

Alfred Takes the Cake

There's an old story that Alfred, on the run in the Somerset marshes, took refuge in the hut of a swineherd. Not knowing who he was, the swineherd's wife gave him the job of watching some cakes she was cooking. Alfred was brooding over plans for reconquering his kingdom and he neglected the cakes and let them burn. He got a severe ticking-off from the angry housewife, who told him he was a careless lout who'd never amount to anything.

A bad cook but a good king, Alfred eventually made a comeback, defeating the Danish King Guthrum at the battle of Ethandune in 878.

Alf's Navy

Alfred was one of the first monarchs to make himself responsible for laying down laws and dispensing justice - an important part of the king's job for many years to come. He also organised a force of ships to patrol the coast and provide an early warning of coming invasions - thus founding the Royal Navy.

Alfred was followed by an fairly obscure collection of kings with names like Edred, Eadwig, Edgar, and the notoriously unready Ethelred. The last two of these Saxon kings deserve a mention.

BREAKFAST, ETHELRED !

UNREADY BREK

EDWARD THE CONFESSOR - 1042-1066

The last surviving son of Ethelred, Edward was pious but feeble. Half-Saxon, half-Norman, he spent his early life in Normandy, and always favoured Norman customs - like washing and shaving - which the sturdy Saxons reckoned to be soft and cissy. Edward failed to provide a proper heir (see earlier) and the throne passed - briefly - to Harold, second son of the powerful and ambitious Earl Godwin.

HAROLD II - 1066

In both looks and character, Harold was the heroic type. A brawny blond-bearded giant, he was noble, brave and generous. He might have made the best English king since Alfred. Unfortunately, his timing was terrible.

No sooner was he on the throne than he had to cope with two invasions at once. The first came in the north, led by his own brother, Tostig (see what I mean about ambitious relatives?) aided by King Harald Hadrada of Norway.

Harold defeated this first invasion in fine style, but then had to dash down south to deal with a second invasion led by William of Normandy.

A Losing Double

Playing two first-division fixtures in swift succession turned out to be a major mistake. Harold's exhausted army was defeated by the away team, and Harold himself was killed.

In later years, William's victory and the events of his reign were commemorated in the world's first comic strip, the famous Bayeux Tapestry. Incidentally, a misreading of the tapestry gave rise to the legend that Harold was killed by an arrow in the eye.

If you look at the picture closely, you can see that it's the next man who got the arrow - Harold was actually killed by a sword. But, like so many historical mistakes, the arrow-in-the-eye version stuck - it seems to be here to stay.

After the battle, Duke William of Normandy was King William I of England.

And this is where our story really starts.

EDWARD THE CONFESSOR
AS A CHILD

THE NORMANS

The Normans

William I - 1066-1087

Once he became King of England William I was flatteringly referred to as William the Conqueror.

In his early days they called him William the Bastard - which he was in every sense of the word.

Romantic Robert

William was the illegitimate son of Robert, Duke of Normandy, and a medieval single mother called Herleve, the daughter of Fulbert, a wealthy tanner of Falaise in Normandy.

Legend says that Robert saw the beautiful Herleve washing clothes in a stream outside his castle and fell madly in love with her. Never one to waste time, Duke Robert, also known as Robert the Devil, whisked her away from the laundry and made her his official mistress. In due course she bore him a son - our future King William.

Unlike some of today's unmarried dads, Robert was a devoted lover and a proud father. On Robert's death, young William inherited the Duchy of Normandy.

A Dangerous Duchy

Inheriting the Duchy was one thing, keeping it quite another. William was illegitimate, he was low-born on his mother's side, and he was only eight years old. Quite a few Norman barons felt the late Robert had made a terrible mistake and that Normandy would be much better off in other hands - like their own.

Herleve, as bright as she was beautiful, promptly married into the nobility, providing herself with a powerful husband and some influential friends.

William grew up under the care of three powerful protectors, the Count of Brittany, the Count of Brionne, and Osbert the Seneschal. All three were assassinated - but somehow young William survived, made tough and cunning by his early dangers.

He grew up strong and determined, a powerful fighter and a born leader with a will - and a fist - of iron. While still in his teens he defeated his cousin Guy of Burgundy, who was trying to steal his dukedom.

A Kingdom for William

With Normandy firmly in his grip, William's ambition started stretching beyond a mere dukedom. In 1053 he married Matilda, daughter of Count Baldwin of Flanders. It just so happened that Matilda was a direct descendant of Alfred the Great...

In 1051 William popped over to England to visit King Edward the Confessor, now his second cousin by marriage. On the strength of this rather faint family connection, the forceful William persuaded the feeble Edward to name him as his successor.

Once his dominating relative was safely back across the Channel, the ever-dithering Edward started having second thoughts. It was true that Edward had no direct heir - but William wasn't the popular choice to fill the vacancy.

As far as the English were concerned, Harold Earl of Wessex, brave, handsome, and above all Saxon, was the man for the job.

Hard Luck for Harold

Then, in 1064, William had an amazing stroke of luck. Earl Harold was shipwrecked on the coast of Normandy. Duke William dashed to the rescue. He took Harold to one of his castles and treated him as an honoured guest. He also made it absolutely clear that if Earl Harold ever expected to see England again, he had to promise to support William's claim to the crown of England once poor old Edward died.

William's Trick

Earl Harold had no choice - not unless he wanted his cross-Channel awayday to last for the rest of his life. Desperate to get back to England, he gave his word. The promise was made over a tapestry-covered chest. When the ceremony was over, William whipped away the cloth - revealing that the chest contained the bones of a saint. If Earl Harold broke his promise, his immortal soul would be in peril.

Harold decided that the crown of England was worth the risk. When Edward died in 1066, Earl Harold was proclaimed king.

Storming Normans

Using Harold's broken promise to bolster his distinctly dodgy claim, William set off across the Channel to conquer England. He took

HAROLD STRIKES A CHICKEN RIGHT BETWEEN THE EYES SHORTLY BEFORE GETTING ONE IN THE EYE HIMSELF.

all the troops he could raise, backed up by a rag-tag of military adventurers, out for what they could get.

What they got was England. Harold, worn out by defeating one invasion, was in no shape to tackle another. He was defeated and killed at the Battle of Hastings.

In 1066, history's most famous date, Duke William of Normandy became King William I of England.

A Stormy Start

William I was crowned in London's Westminster Abbey on Christmas Day that same year. The new king's reign got off to a stormy start. The shouts of rejoicing from inside the Cathedral alarmed the Norman guards stationed outside. Deciding that an instant rebellion had broken out, they promptly set about the local Saxons. In no time at all a fine old battle was under way. The newly-crowned King William had to dash out of the Abbey to calm things down.

A Rebellious Kingdom

The new king's reign carried on as it had begun. Although the south-east was pretty settled, rebellions broke out all over the place. It took until 1068 to settle the south-west, and in 1069 William defeated yet another rebellion in the north.

It was a tricky few years. William and his armies marched and fought up and down the country, defeating rebels and building massive stone castles to hold down the land they'd (just about) conquered. As Rudyard Kipling puts it:

'Never was a blacksmith like our Norman king

England's being hammered, hammered, hammered into line.'

The heroic Hereward the Wake held out the longest, leading an uprising in the Isle of Ely. But even Hereward was finally defeated by 1071.

All over England, Saxon lords were replaced by Norman barons.

William Takes Stock

In 1085 William ordered a kind of stocktaking of his kingdom. This massive survey, known as the Domesday Book, is an astonishing tribute to his thoroughness and determination.

Even with England (relatively) peaceful, William's troubles weren't over. He still had his Duchy of Normandy to worry about. With William away in England, the King of France and the Count of Anjou promptly started trying to snaffle his dukedom, helped eagerly by Robert, William's eldest son. (Those medieval family values strike again!)

William spent much of the rest of his reign fighting to hang on to England without losing Normandy in the process. It was the death of him in the end.

The Last Battle

In 1087 William was still at war with the King of France.

(It wasn't so much that the King was trying to steal William's dukedom - that was only to be expected. What really enraged William was the fact that the French king had been making rude remarks about William's spreading waistline.)

The French had been raiding into Normandy, and William struck back by sacking the French city of Maintes. Although he was getting a bit past this sort of thing, he led the attack in person. Charging ahead with his victorious troops, William's horse stumbled and he was badly thrown. Since he was a sizable chap by now - there was some truth in the French king's remarks - William came down hard, suffering internal injuries from which he later died.

One King for England

William had succeeded in uniting England under one ruler - even if he'd grabbed the kingdom on dubious grounds and held it down by force of arms.

The anonymous author of the Anglo-Saxon Chronicle, the main history of the time, said William was, 'A man of great wisdom and power, and surpassed in honour and strength all those who had gone before him. Though stern beyond measure to those who opposed his will, he was kind to those good men who loved God.'

A fighter all his life, he was well-named The Conqueror.

WILLIAM II - 1087-1100

As so often happens with the sons of great men, the next king turned out to be a bit of a let-down.

You'll remember that the expected heir, Robert, had rebelled against his father. William forgave him and left him the Duchy of Normandy - but he left England to his second son, William, known as William Rufus, because of his red hair and red face.

Although he was a good soldier, William Rufus lacked his father's skill as a ruler. In moral matters he had an evil reputation, and he was unpopular with the Church, who disapproved strongly of his lifestyle.

Gay Times at Court

William of Malmesbury, a historian of the time, said that in William Rufus's court it was the fashion for young men 'to rival women in delicacy of person, to mince their gait, to walk with loose gestures...'

Reading between the medieval lines it seems very probable that William Rufus was gay. He certainly showed no interest in women and he never married.

William Rufus also quarrelled with Anselm, the much-loved Archbishop of Canterbury, who wanted to reform the Church. The king didn't agree. He forced Anselm to leave the country and grabbed the Archbishop's money as well.

The good old Anglo-Saxon Chronicle gives William Rufus a very bad press. 'He was very harsh and fierce in his rule over his realm...everything that was hateful to God and to righteous man was the daily practice in this land during his reign. Therefore he was hated by almost all his people...'

A Suspicious Death

As might be expected with such an unpopular king, William Rufus died in suspicious circumstances.

He was hunting in the New Forest with his younger brother Henry and an assortment of knights. The story is that the king was chasing a stag, accompanied by a knight called Sir Walter Tyrel. The king shot an arrow at the stag and missed. He yelled out to Tyrel to shoot.

Tyrel shot - missing the stag but killing the king.

Today a tale like that would spawn as many conspiracy theories as the Kennedy assassination.

Henry Takes Over

There's some suspicion that brother Henry, next in line for the throne, might just possibly have been involved - it was in the family tradition after all. Henry certainly seized the Royal Treasury with suspicious speed, straight after Rufus's death. And he *was* very generous to Tyrel's family once he became king...

However, since Rufus was so unpopular, everyone was quite happy to accept the official account. The body was chucked into a peasant's cart and taken to Winchester Cathedral, dripping blood all the way. The clergy refused to perform a service, and the royal corpse was hastily buried under the Cathedral tower.

Next year the tower fell down...

HENRY I - 1100-1135

Henry I was a much more English king than his father and brother. Youngest of the Conqueror's three sons, he was the only one born in England.

Henry inherited the dash and decision of his father. Straight after his brother's death he shot off to Winchester, secured the Royal Treasury, and got as many of the nobles as were around to elect him king. Then he galloped off to London and got himself crowned.

Henry had inherited his father's political cunning as well. As soon as he was king, he took steps to regain the popularity Rufus had lost. He issued a citizen's charter, promising a back-to-basics return to his father's ways of 'good governance' and justice for all. He recalled Archbishop Anselm, banished by his brother, and restored him to his place as Archbishop of Canterbury.

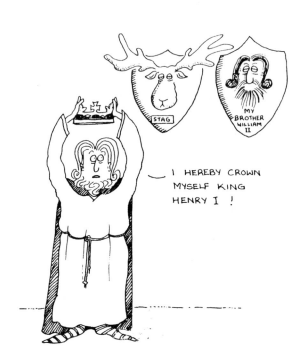

Edith becomes Matilda

Next Henry looked round for a suitable wife. He chose Edith, the eldest daughter of Malcolm Canmore, King of Scots, renaming her Matilda in honour of his mother - which pleased his Norman barons. The new queen was a descendant of Alfred the Great, so Henry's Saxon subjects approved of the marriage as well.

Big Brother Again

Henry's big brother Robert, now Duke of Normandy, was still giving trouble. Having failed to grab the throne from his dad, he now tried to take it away from his younger brother. In 1101 he invaded England, only to be soundly beaten. After his defeat he was forced to sign the Treaty of Alton, confirming Henry as King of England, Robert as Duke of Normandy.

If Robert had had any sense he'd have left things that way. He'd had two unsuccessful goes at grabbing the crown by now. But in 1106 he tried again. It was a case of third time unlucky. Once again Henry defeated him. Fed up with family feuds, Henry took away Robert's Duchy of Normandy, and locked him up in Cardiff Castle for the rest of his life. He bestowed Normandy upon William, his beloved son.

Family Problems

Like so many monarchs, Henry was unlucky in the matter of heirs. His first child died in infancy and William was drowned in 1120, returning from Normandy. A drunken pilot ran the ship on the rocks.

Henry's third child, Matilda, was a girl. As soon as she was old enough, he married her off to the German Emperor, Henry V. Henry's wife Matilda had died in 1118, and although Henry married again, the marriage was childless. In 1126 Henry named his now-widowed daughter, the Empress Matilda, as his successor.

A Fishy Fate

Though his reign was fairly peaceful, Henry had ended up with the old problem of ruling both England and Normandy. He was always nipping to and fro between the two keeping things quiet. In the end it wasn't fighting that finished off Henry - it was French cuisine. In 1135 he was back in Normandy, visiting his hunting lodge near Gisors. There, according to Henry of Huntingdon, a historian of the time: 'He devoured lampreys, which always disagreed with him.' (My dictionary defines lampreys as: 'an eel-like fish with a sucker mouth'. Yuk!)

'He was *excessively* fond of them,' says the disapproving historian. 'When his physicians forbade him to eat them, the king did not heed their advice!'

This 'surfeit of lampreys' was followed by a severe attack of food-poisoning, from which the king eventually died - finished off by the fish course.

ANOTHER COURSE OF LAMPREYS FOR HENRY I —
OR COULD IT BE A 'CURSE' OF LAMPREYS ?

A Respectable Reign

During his reign Henry I kept the peace and imposed law and order, often with a heavy hand. He founded the Court of the Exchequer to sort out Crown finances, and brought in many useful administrative reforms, including a system of travelling justices. He even founded the first zoo...

The Anglo-Saxon Chronicle gives him a respectable end-of-reign report.

'He was a good man and was held in great awe. In his days, no man dared wrong another. He made peace for man and beast.'

STEPHEN - 1135-1154

King Henry's peace didn't long survive his reign.

Once again, the trouble was the succession. King Henry had chosen his daughter Matilda, but the male-chauvinist barons decided they'd sooner have a chap. Defying the royal will, they picked Henry's highly popular nephew, Count Stephen of Blois.

In 1126 Stephen had been one of the first barons to swear allegiance to Matilda as his future queen.

In 1128 the widowed Matilda had re-married. Her new husband was Geoffrey, Count of Anjou. In 1133, when their son Henry was born, Stephen renewed his oath of loyalty to Matilda. However, none of these promises prevented him from belting straight over from Boulogne as soon as the king was dead and accepting the throne from the rebellious barons.

Matilda Fights Back

The Empress Matilda, who'd been her father's candidate for the job, put up a tremendous squawk when the sneaky Stephen took the throne. But Stephen had secured the support of the Pope. He'd also got his hands on the royal treasury, and began spreading it about, bribing the greedy barons for their support.

Matilda, however, had some influential friends of her own. In 1139 she landed in England to enforce her claim. She was supported by her half-brother, the Earl of Gloucester, and by a number of other barons.

For the next fourteen years England was torn by civil war.

(Crime novel note: the popular 'Brother Cadfael' series of crime stories by Ellis Peters, about a medieval monk who doubles as a detective, is set in the time of the Stephen and Matilda civil war.)

The War Goes On

The war dragged on and on, with first one side then the other gaining the upper hand.

In 1141, Stephen was defeated at Lincoln and imprisoned at Bristol. Bishop Henry, Stephen's brother, turned against his defeated relative. The unbrotherly bishop declared Stephen deposed and proclaimed Matilda queen.

Undeterred, Stephen's supporters fought on without him. They captured Matilda's top supporter, the Earl of Gloucester - and swapped him for Stephen.

Stephen promptly had himself re-crowned.

The struggle went on.

To add to Stephen's troubles, Matilda's husband, Geoffrey of Anjou, captured Normandy in 1144.

In an attempt to secure the succession, Stephen had his son Eustace crowned in 1152 - but the Pope refused to allow it.

Matilda Retires

Matilda was getting on a bit by now, so she retired to Normandy. But it didn't help Stephen. By now Matilda's son Henry was grown up and raring to go. He landed in England in 1153 and all Matilda's supporters flocked to join him.

Stephen's Deal

By now Stephen had finally had enough. His wife and son were both dead - he didn't even have an heir to inherit the throne. To avoid further fighting, Stephen made a deal with young Henry. In the Treaty of Westminster they agreed that Stephen could keep the throne for his own lifetime, and that Henry should become king after Stephen's death. Henry didn't have long to wait. Next year Stephen was struck down by appendicitis and died.

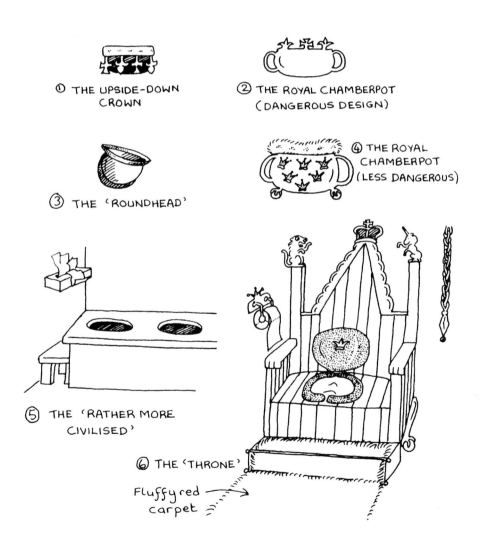

CHANGING STYLES OF ROYAL LOO

① THE UPSIDE-DOWN CROWN

② THE ROYAL CHAMBERPOT (DANGEROUS DESIGN)

③ THE 'ROUNDHEAD'

④ THE ROYAL CHAMBERPOT (LESS DANGEROUS)

⑤ THE 'RATHER MORE CIVILISED'

⑥ THE 'THRONE'

Fluffy red carpet

THE PLANTAGENETS

THE PLANTAGENETS

Although Henry II's claim to the throne came through his mother, Matilda, his father, Geoffrey, Count of Anjou, was to give the new dynasty its name. Geoffrey had been nicknamed *Plantagenet*, because of his habit of wearing a sprig of flowering broom (Latin name: *Planta genista*). The name stuck, and in time the family became known as the Plantagenets...

HENRY II - 1154-1189

The new line got off to a good start with the most impressive monarch since the Conqueror himself.

Henry II was a lion of a man, strong and handsome, brave and clever, with a forceful personality and a fiery temper. Despite his many good qualities, Henry had more than his share of troubles. Some came from that temper of his - but quite a few of them came through his wife, Eleanor of Aquitaine.

Here was a royal marriage that *really* had problems - Charles and Di aren't even in the same league.

ELEANOR AND HENRY II FALL OUT (AGAIN)

The Affairs of Eleanor

Eleanor had originally married King Louis VII of France. Never a girl to sit at home with her embroidery, she accompanied him to Palestine on the Crusades - the unending attempts by various Christian kings to recapture the Holy Land from the 'infidel'

Saracens. There she is said to have had a number of scandalous affairs - including one with the Saracen Emperor Saladin himself. (This is roughly equivalent to Maggie having a fling with Saddam Hussein.) Louis felt this was carrying diplomatic activity too far. When they got home again he had the marriage annulled.

Eleanor Scores Again

Free again, Eleanor lost no time in seducing the future King of England. Henry at that time was Duke of Normandy and Count of Anjou. They married in 1152 when Henry was nineteen and Eleanor thirty. They had five sons and three daughters, and fought like tigers all their lives.

In the later years of the marriage Henry got very fed up with the fiery Eleanor, who kept stirring up their sons to rebel against him. (Not that they needed much encouragement.) To get a bit of peace he locked her up in a castle in France.

(Film note: the film 'The Lion in Winter', with Peter O'Toole as Henry and Katharine Hepburn as Eleanor, gives an entertaining, and fairly accurate, picture of Plantaganet family values.)

Henry Takes Hold

As soon as he was king, Henry set to work clearing up the mess left by years of civil war. He destroyed the castles of the rebellious barons, replacing them with bigger and better castles of his own.

In 1162 Henry appointed his friend Thomas Becket Archbishop of Canterbury, hoping Thomas would help him to reform the Church. He regained the northern territories of England from Scotland, invaded Wales, and made plans to conquer Ireland.

Henry also tried to limit the powers of the Church to deal with crimes committed by the clergy. (They had some very suspect priests and crooked clerics in those days.) This led to a fierce quarrel with Becket, who was taking his duties as Archbishop rather more seriously than Henry had intended.

The hot-tempered king was outraged that his old friend dared to defy him. In 1164 Becket was forced into exile - and Henry seized the archbishop's revenues.

In 1166 Henry sent a force under the Earl of Pembroke to settle Ireland - some hopes - beginning a history of trouble that's still going on today.

Murder in the Cathedral

In 1170 pressure from the Pope forced Henry to try to make up his quarrel with Becket. The exile came home - but he was still defiant. Soon king and archbishop quarrelled yet again, and Thomas went off to Canterbury.

The king said, 'Will no-one rid me of this turbulent priest?'

In all probability he didn't really mean it - but four of his knights took him at his word. Jealous of Becket's influence and keen to please the king, they rode off to Canterbury and murdered the archbishop in his own cathedral.

(Literary note: See T.S. Eliot's famous verse-play called, surprisingly enough, 'Murder in the Cathedral'.)

Henry's Penance

The murder certainly didn't bring Henry any benefits. To obtain the Pope's forgiveness he had to give way on everything in his dispute with the Church, and do public penance for Becket's death. (Just to rub it in, the Church made Becket an official saint in 1173.)

Family Feuds

Henry's later years were beset with problems. The sheer size of his Anglo-French kingdom made it hard to rule, and he was always dashing about from one place to another.

But most of his troubles were family ones. His sons, Henry, Richard and Geoffrey, all led armed rebellions against him - egged on by their mother Eleanor, who was still making mischief even in exile. When Henry heard that John, his youngest and favourite son, had joined the rebels, the news broke his heart.

Henry Fights On

Old and weary by now, Henry battled on. In 1189 he was in France for a summit meeting with King Philip. Although ill with fever, Henry insisted on attending the meeting. As he rode to meet the French king, a thunderclap startled Henry's horse and he was badly thrown. He was carried to the Castle of Chinon where he lay dying.

Even on his deathbed he had little peace. A deputation of monks from Canterbury turned up, pestering him for more concessions. Henry asked to be carried to the altar of the castle church. He died there in a fit of rage, calling down heaven's vengeance on his rebellious sons...

A King to Remember

At its peak Henry II's empire took in England, Wales, Ireland, and large chunks of France - Normandy, Anjou and Aquitaine. Tough, energetic and athletic, he loved war and hunting, but he was a scholar and an intellectual as well.

During his reign he reformed and overhauled the English legal system. The law itself, the administration of the law courts, the maintenance of law and order, all benefited by his attention. Trial by jury was first introduced during Henry's reign.

Despite the turmoil and unhappiness of his later years, and his really horrendous family life, Henry II was one of the greatest of our kings.

RICHARD I - 1189-1199

Henry's eldest son, also called Henry, died before his father. On King Henry's death the throne passed to Richard, the next brother in line.

Richard I, also known as Richard the Lionheart, is one king who's always enjoyed a really good image. He owes it
to all those Robin Hood movies, starring everyone from Errol Flynn to Kevin Costner. You all know the story...

RICHARD I

Robin of Sherwood

While brave King Richard is away at the Crusades, the kingdom goes to pot under the rule of his bad brother John. He and his wicked henchman the Sheriff of Nottingham (Boo! Hiss!) increase everyone's income tax and make the lives of the miserable peasants even more of a misery than usual.

An unjustly outlawed nobleman takes the name Robin Hood. With his girlfriend, Maid Marion, he leads a Lincoln Green Party resistance movement from Sherwood Forest, robbing the rich to feed the poor, refusing to pay the hovel tax and the VAT on venison. The story ends happily when good King Richard comes home, sees off his bad brother, and gives Robin back his earldom - after which everyone lives happily ever after.

All good stuff - but it wasn't quite like that.

EEK! IT IS A
REAL MOUSE!

An Absentee King

Leaving aside the purely legendary Robin Hood, Richard's only real distinction as King of England is that he was hardly ever around. He was only in the country twice during his ten-year reign, once for two months, later for three.

The Lionheart part of the legend is true enough. Richard was a born soldier, never happier than when in battle. He was also a keen Crusader, sworn to dedicate his life to the recapture of the Holy Land from the Saracens.

In 1189 Richard was on the continent when he heard the news of his father's death. He set off for home, stopping off in Rouen to get himself made Duke of Normandy. He returned to England, was crowned in Westminster, raised as much cash as he could and went straight back to Normandy. From there he set off for Palestine, accompanied by King Philip of France.

BUT, SIRE, IT IS A STONE LION !

RICHARD THE LIONHEART

A Marriage is Arranged

On the way to the Crusades, Richard stopped off in Cyprus to marry a Spanish princess, Berengaria of Navarre, a purely political affair arranged by his mother Eleanor.

This was another bizarre royal marriage that makes today's scandals seem tame. Despite his excessively macho behaviour, Richard was actually gay - the bride's main attraction was that she was the sister of one of Richard's old boyfriends.

Not surprisingly, there were no children.

Berengaria was crowned Queen of England - but she outdid even her absentee king of a husband by never setting foot in the country at all!

An Unlucky Crusade

The Crusade didn't quite work out too well either.

In 1191 Richard and his allies were only twelve miles from Jerusalem. Unfortunately they never got any further. The Crusaders fixed up a truce with Saladin, and in 1192 Richard set off for home.

It was an unlucky journey. Richard got shipwrecked in the Adriatic and had to do the rest of the journey by land. This involved crossing the territory of the Duke of Austria - whom Richard had insulted back in the Holy Land.

The Duke, who still bore a grudge, slung Richard into prison.

At this point we get another romantic legend. Richard had a faithful minstrel called Blondel, a sort of medieval Beatle. When Richard went missing, Blondel went on a European tour, singing Richard's favourite ditty outside every castle he could find - until he heard Richard singing back. It's a good story, and might even be true.

Home and Away

Once Richard's whereabouts were known, poor old England had to fork up the ransom. Somehow the money was raised and in 1194 Richard returned home. When he got back he found his bad brother John was rifling the royal treasury for his own benefit, and making plans to grab the throne as well.

Like a lot of rogues, John was something of a charmer. Somehow he managed to convince his brave-but-dim big brother that he hadn't really meant any harm, and Richard forgave him.

Because of Richard's delayed homecoming the King of France got back first - and lost no time in trying to grab Normandy and Richard's other French territories.

Happy at the thought of of a bit more fighting, Richard set off for France to sort him out. He spent the next few years trying to regain his lost lands.

A Bolt from the Blue

In 1199 Richard was laying siege to the disputed town of Chalus when he was struck in the shoulder by a cross-bow bolt shot from the walls. Macho as ever, Richard neglected the wound, refusing to have it treated till he'd captured the town, which he did a few days later. His physician made a botch-up of the arrow-extraction, the wound became infected, and Richard died.

(His angry barons executed the physician - things were tough in the National Health Service in those days.)

Despite his colourful career, Richard had very little impact on events in England - simply because he was never there. He left no heir. On his deathbed he named his brother John as his successor.

JOHN - 1199-1216

Just as popular history makes Richard a hero, it stamps John a villain. To be fair, he lived in exceptionally difficult times - and he did

JOHN AND ISABELLA HAVING A PLEASANT FAMILY CHAT

have some good qualities. He was keen on taking baths, for instance - a rare virtue in those days.

John started out as the spoiled baby of the family. The youngest son, he was a favourite with his father King Henry, his mother Eleanor, and his brother Richard, who always forgave his various bits of villainy.

Unlike his brothers John inherited no territory of his own. He was mockingly nicknamed John Lackland.

When Richard became king, he gave John a small county in Normandy called Mortain, and arranged a marriage for him with an English heiress called Isabella of Gloucester. John wasn't mad about Mortain, or about Isabella either, but for the moment he had to settle for both.

John's Opportunity

King Richard went off to the Crusades, leaving a Norman called Longchamp in charge as his Chancellor. The English barons resented this, and John seized his opportunity. Taking advantage of their discontent, he made himself their leader. He raised an army to seize London, and Chancellor Longchamp fled disguised as a woman.

The disguise must have been a bit too convincing. When Longchamp was at Dover, waiting for a ship, he took the fancy of a passing sailor. So determined were the advances of the randy mariner that Longchamp had to remove his disguise in self-protection - and was captured by John's men. John was so delighted by the story that he ordered Longchamp released. A villain he may have been, but he had a sense of humour.

Richard's return put a stop to John's schemes to seize power and he was forced to bide his time...

Duke - and King

As soon as he heard the news of Richard's death, John went to Rouen and had himself installed as Duke of Normandy. Unlucky as ever, he dropped the ceremonial spear during the ceremony.

People said it was a bad omen - and given what happened later, maybe it was! John crossed over to England and was crowned in Westminster Cathedral.

There was actually another candidate with a better claim to the throne. Arthur, Duke of Brittany, was the son of John's now-dead elder brother, Geoffrey. Technically he was ahead of John in the line of succession. But Arthur was only eleven - he could easily be pushed aside.

Changing Isabellas

John's next step was to get rid of his unwanted wife by having the marriage annulled. He married another Isabella, the twelve-year-old Isabella of Angouleme, with whom he had fallen madly in love. In spite of this it turned out to be yet another rocky royal marriage, with a good deal of infidelity on both sides.

Exit Arthur

A few years later, John started worrying about his young rival again. Duke Arthur was already fifteen. John decided it might be better if the lad never saw sixteen... In 1203 Duke Arthur was murdered at Rouen. No-one had any doubts about who was behind it - certainly not King Philip of France. Combining a high moral tone with self-interest, he decided it was time to take back Normandy. In 1204 French troops entered Rouen.

Problems with the Pope

Having quarrelled with the French king, John now fell out with the Pope - a bad move in those days. He refused to accept the Pope's nominee, Stephen Langton, as Archbishop of Canterbury.

In 1208 the Pope excommunicated him - and laid a Papal interdict on the whole country. They took their religion seriously in those days - to most people this meant that both king and country were damned.

By 1213 John was forced to submit. Before the Pope would lift the ban, John had to surrender his kingdom, and accept it back as the Pope's servant.

Defeated by the French

Beaten by the Pope, John decided to have a go at getting his French lands back and invaded France. But John lacked his brother's military genius. In 1214 he was defeated at Bouvines.

The Rebellious Barons

There was worse to come. Back home the barons, fed up with John's misrule, were ganging up on him, under the leadership of Stephen Langton. When John got home from France, he was immediately surrounded by bolshy barons. In 1215 they took him to Runnymede, a small island in the Thames, and forced him to sign something called Magna Carta - the 'great charter'.

The Great Charter

Magna Carta limited the king's powers to tax the barons, and guaranteed the rights of the Church and the City corporations. It also laid down that no man was to be arrested or imprisoned except according to the judgement of his peers and under the laws of the land.

Magna Carta is immensely important as a symbol of freedom. The very idea that the powers of a king *could* be checked was something new. It was the start of a long power-struggle, first between king and nobles, later between nobles and parliament.

King John hated Magna Carta. He'd only signed the rotten thing under threat, and he was determined to tear it up just as soon as he could. He made up with his old enemy the Pope - who didn't like all these new-fangled ideas either - and got his backing to raise an army to crush the rebellious barons.

The French Invade

The barons turned to France for help, sending for Louis the Dauphin - nearly all French royals seemed to be called Louis - heir to the throne of France. Louis landed in England and the rebel barons promised him the English throne, if he dealt with John first. There followed a year of civil war with lots of indecisive skirmishing and much marching up and down.

Unlucky John

John's luck ran out again. In 1216 he and his army were crossing the Wash, a huge river estuary between Norfolk and Lincolnshire. Some fool misread the tide table, the sea rushed in and John and his army were washed away, bag and baggage. John survived but he lost his crown and most of the royal regalia.

Damp, dripping and depressed, John staggered out of the water and fell ill with a fever. According to a disapproving historian of the time, 'He aggravated his illness by disgusting gluttony, for that night, by indulging too freely in peaches and copious draughts of new cider, he greatly increased his feverishness.'

With a staggering hangover and a severe case of the trots to add to his troubles, poor old John was carried to Newark Castle, where he died a day or two later.

He was buried in Worcester Cathedral. At his own request, he was buried, dressed as a monk, close to the tomb of a saint. Maybe he planned to sneak into Heaven in disguise...

A ROYAL SNACK FOR JOHN —
NOT SURPRISING HE GOT ILL !

Bad King John

It's hard to find something good to say about bad King John. He had charm and a sense of humour, at least when he was young, and he was capable of occasional acts of kindness.

As a villain he was dead unlucky - all his evil schemes went badly wrong. But he did achieve two useful things, both of them against his will.

By losing Normandy he freed later kings, for a time, from the near-impossible task of trying to rule two countries at once.

And by signing Magna Carta, however unwillingly, he laid the foundations of the democracy of today.

HENRY III - 1216-1272

Something John the Bad did manage to do was provide the kingdom with an heir, even if the candidate was still a bit young for the job.

When John came to his expected bad end, Queen Isabella and her children were at Gloucester. There were five children, two boys and three girls. The eldest boy, Henry, was now the new king, Henry III. He was nine years old.

A child-king is always a dodgy proposition, but there was no alternative. With Louis and his French knights and various rebel barons rampaging around it was thought best to get the boy king crowned straight away.

The Cheap Coronation

It was a bit of a cut-rate coronation. There wasn't even a proper crown - John had lost it in the Wash. London was in the hands of the rebels, so Westminster Cathedral and the remaining royal regalia just weren't available.

Young Henry had to be crowned at Gloucester, using one of his Mum's gold bracelets as a temporary crown. However, the hurried ceremony achieved its purpose. The quickness of the coronation took the rebels by surprise and the revolt folded up.

Royal Guardians

The boy king was put in the charge of William Marshal, Earl of Pembroke, who acted as Regent, ruling the country till the king grew up. A fine soldier and a skilled politician, Marshal chased off Louis and the French, and brought the rebel barons back under control.

William Marshal died in 1219 and was replaced by Hubert de Burgh. The other main guardian was Peter des Roches, Bishop of Winchester. Hubert and the Bishop became deadly rivals.

Crowned Again

In 1220 Henry was crowned again, this time in Westminster Cathedral, with the full ceremony and all the proper gear.

Things had gone well enough while William Marshal was running things, and Hubert de Burgh didn't do badly at first. It was only when Henry grew up and took over that things started going wrong. The new king was weak-willed, indecisive and easily led.

Henry III started ruling in earnest in 1227 when he was twenty. Hubert de Burgh, still influential, was given the job of Justiciar, the state official in charge of law and order. The Bishop of Winchester, his old rival, suddenly decided he'd be safer back in France.

French Friends

Then Hubert de Burgh was caught with his fingers in the royal till, and was thrown into jail. The Bishop of Winchester came back to England and Henry gave him the job of Treasurer. Unfortunately the bishop brought lots of French friends and relations with him, giving them all the top jobs.

The English didn't like this much, and they eventually rebelled. The king was forced to dismiss the bishop and his French followers. But things still didn't improve.

A French Princess

In 1236 Henry married a French princess, Eleanor of Provence. Pretty soon all *her* friends and relations started flooding into the top jobs - three of her uncles became King's ministers.

Foreign advisors, high taxes and inefficient rule put King Henry low in the popularity polls. An unsuccessful foreign policy didn't help either. A military expedition to recover the lost French territories turned out a complete failure.

Rebellion Again

After twenty years of increasing discontent, there was another rebellion. It was led by an able and energetic Frenchman, Simon de Montfort, Earl of Leicester, King Henry's brother-in-law.

De Montfort and the barons forced Henry to sign the Provisions of Oxford, a sort of Magna Carta Mark 2, limiting royal power.

Henry signed, then, typically, changed his mind, rejecting the agreement. The barons rebelled - again - and in 1264 civil war broke out. King Henry was defeated and captured at the battle of Lewes. He was forced to agree to rule with the help of a parliament and a council of barons.

The Birth of Parliament

In 1265 de Montfort summoned a Great Council - the first English parliament - an assembly of lords, bishops and knights. There were even burgesses, officials representing the big towns - the first time ordinary people got any sort of say at all.

But the defeated King Henry had an ace in the hole. His eldest son, Edward, had grown up to be a strong and determined leader, and a very good soldier, unlike his indecisive Dad.

A Family Victory

Carrying on the struggle, even though Dad had surrendered, Prince Edward defeated the rebel barons at Evesham. Their leader de Montfort was killed, and Edward, and Richard Duke of Cornwall the King's brother, made peace with the remaining rebels.

Poor old Henry didn't count for much after that. The kingdom was ruled by his son and his brother, both far better at the job than the real king.

An Ineffective King

Henry turned increasingly to religion and became, according to the historian Holinshed, 'somewhat crasie'. He died at the Palace of Westminster in 1272.

Not a bad man, but definitely a bad king, the ineffective Henry managed to reign for an amazing fifty-six years - though of course, he'd started young.

Just as with his father John, the most important event of Henry III's reign happened against his will.

Like Magna Carta, the defeated de Montfort's Great Council was another stumbling step towards democracy...

EDWARD I - 1272-1307

The hereditary system is always a bit of a lottery. This time it came up with another winner.

Edward I was tall (he was nicknamed 'Longshanks'), strong and handsome, strong-willed but willing to take advice.

Unlike so many royals, Edward enjoyed a long and happy marriage. As a lad of fifteen, he went on a trip to Spain. Not only was he knighted by King Alfonso X, he ended up marrying Alfonso's half-sister, Eleanor the Infanta of Castile.

THE FIRST ROYAL VARIETY PERFORMANCE

When the royal couple came home, Edward's English subjects had terrible trouble with Eleanor's Spanish title. They couldn't get their tongues round 'Infanta de Castile' so they turned it into 'Elephant and Castle', naming a pub and an area of London after her.

A Happy Marriage

Edward and Eleanor were a devoted couple. Edward was so fond of his wife that he took her away on Crusades. Eleanor was equally keen on her royal husband. She even saved his life by sucking the poison from his wounded arm, when a local assassin tried to polish him off with a poisoned dagger.

A Troubled Reign

It's as well Edward had a happy home life. His kingly career was anything but peaceful. Besides battling in the Crusades, a sort of hobby for kings of the time, Edward had to fight the usual rebellious barons. He also spent a lot of time trying to sort out the Welsh and the Scots, both of whom had some strange objection to becoming British.

Edward did pretty well with the Welsh, defeating their last two native princes, Llewelyn and David.

A Prince for Wales

In 1284 Edward and Eleanor, who was heavily pregnant by now, visited Wales to try to win over the recently conquered Welsh. Edward promised the Welsh nobles a ruler who'd been born in Wales and didn't speak a word of English. When the Welsh nobles gathered to meet their new ruler, Edward said, 'Here is your new Prince of Wales!' He held up his baby son, who'd just been born in Caernarfon Castle.

Ever since then the king's first-born son has born that title.

The Stubborn Scots

The Scots proved a much tougher proposition. At first Edward had a certain amount of success. He won a major victory at Falkirk in 1298 when he defeated the Scottish leader Wallace and swiped Scotland's Coronation Stone, the famous Stone of Scone. He took it to Westminster Abbey and had a special chair made to contain it. Since then nearly all English sovereigns have been crowned in this Coronation Chair.

Undaunted, the Scots soon came up with another leader, a brilliant soldier called Robert the Bruce. (He's the one who's said to have learned patience from watching a spider patiently building its web.)

Successfully continuing the struggle against the invading Sassenachs, Robert the Bruce was crowned King of Scotland at Scone in 1306 - even though there was no Stone of Scone for him to sit on.

Edward tried so hard to clobber the stubborn Scots into submission that he became known as 'The Hammer of the Scots'. In 1307 he was travelling north to have another bash at them when he fell ill and died.

SOME ROYAL BEASTS MISBEHAVING

A Model Monarch

Edward I has been called the model medieval king. A fine soldier and a skilled statesman, he called frequent councils, saying 'What touches all should be approved by all.'

These councils, or 'parliaments' as they came to be called, were the beginnings of the elected parliaments of today.

EDWARD II - 1307-1327

Being king in medieval times was like managing the England football team - if you didn't produce plenty of away wins against those fiendish foreigners you were in trouble. Edward I had given his subjects what they wanted. But war is always an expensive hobby. Edward's triumphs meant higher taxes. The barons were muttering again, and Edward II inherited their discontent.

Unfortunately, he wasn't the man his father was - in more ways than one. Youngest, and only survivor of Edward I's four sons, Edward was brought up by his mother and sisters. With his father away fighting all the time, Edward was definitely deprived when it came to male bonding. When he did find a boy friend, so to speak, the choice was an unfortunate one.

Gorgeous Gaveston

Piers Gaveston was a handsome young Frenchman, famous for the extravagance of his costume and the sharpness of his tongue. Not only did he out-dress the other nobles, he made up rude nick- names for them as well - rash policy in a court full of bad-tempered barons. Edward's father was so worried about Gaveston's influence over his son that he banished him from the kingdom. But as soon as Edward became king he called Gaveston back again, and created him Duke of Cornwall.

Piers in Charge

When Edward II sailed for Boulogne in 1308 to marry Isabella of France, he left Piers Gaveston in charge of the country. When the couple came home after the wedding, Gaveston greeted the king with such an extravagant display of affection that the new Queen was very upset, and her accompanying uncles extremely suspicious.

Things didn't improve at the banquet to welcome the happy couple home. Gaveston turned up in an outfit of purple velvet and pearls, outshining the sovereign himself, and treated the King's relatives with such disrespect that there was nearly a punch-up. To make matters worse he completely screwed up the arrangements for the banquet itself. The food arrived late, badly-cooked and cold, and the feast didn't get going until after dark - not one of our more successful royal weddings.

Gaveston Goes Too Far

After this rocky start, the royal marriage stood little chance of success. Isabella did her wifely duty however, bearing Edward a son, also called Edward, in 1312. Another son and two daughters were to follow.

Feelings against Piers Gaveston soon rose so high that Edward sent him off to Ireland until things cooled down. But he couldn't live without his dear Piers for long, and soon Piers was back at court, annoying everyone more than ever. In 1312 the Earl of Warwick - nicknamed by Gaveston 'The Black Dog of Arden' - decided enough was enough. He kidnapped Gaveston and had him murdered.

Another Crack at the Scots

King Edward decided he'd better try to retrieve a bit of the royal reputation. What he needed was a successful war. He decided it was time to complete the conquest of Scotland.

Robert the Bruce must have learned a thing or two from that spider after all. In 1314 he totally defeated Edward at the Battle of Bannockburn, ensuring Scotland's independence for hundreds of years to come.

The Despicable Despensers

Poor Edward became more unpopular than ever. It didn't help matters when he took a new favourite, Hugh Despenser, son of the Earl of Winchester. Despenser had first gained the King's favour by supporting Piers Gaveston. Now Hugh and his father took Gaveston's place as the royal favourites.

Love in the Tower

Not surprisingly, the neglected Queen looked for consolation, turning to Roger Mortimer, one of the King's enemies. Mortimer was arrested for high treason and was thrown into the Tower of London, condemned to death. The Queen visited him and they fell in love - an early example of a prison-visitor romance.

In 1323 Isabella helped her lover to escape from the Tower and flee to France. The Despensers used the opportunity to exploit the split between Edward and the Queen. In 1324 they persuaded Edward to confiscate her estates.

Isabella's Army

Understandably cheesed-off, Queen Isabella left England, taking her eldest son with her. She joined her lover Mortimer in France - and set about raising an army.

By now the barons had had more than enough of Edward too, and civil war broke out in England. When Isabella and her army landed in 1326 many of the rebellious barons rallied to her support. In 1327 Edward was defeated. The Despensers were imprisoned and Edward forced to abdicate in favour of his fifteen-year-old son.

The deposed Edward was imprisoned in Berkeley Castle. Shortly afterwards he was murdered by his gaolers in circumstances of shocking brutality. Isabella and Mortimer had ordered that there were to be no external marks of violence on the body. He was killed with a red-hot poker in a way you don't want to know about. His terrible death ended a sad and unsuccessful reign.

QUEEN ISABELLA SET ABOUT RAISING
AN ARMY

EDWARD III - 1327-1377

For the early years of Edward's reign the young king was pretty much a puppet in the hands of his mother and her lover Roger Mortimer. In 1328 they married him off to Philippa of Hainault. Bride and groom were both little more than children, not uncommon in the royal marriages of those days.

Edward, however, didn't take after his weak, unfortunate father - he was more like his tough and capable grandfather. Three years later, Edward felt strong enough to seize power. Ignoring his mother's cry of 'Spare sweet Mortimer!' he arrested Roger Mortimer and executed him. He treated his mum more kindly, shutting her up in Castle Rising in Norfolk and even visiting her occasionally.

Edward Fights Back

Edward found himself faced with trouble on all sides. The barons were grumbling as usual, the French were attacking his possessions in France, and the Scots were sewing their porridge oats as well, prowling the border and looking for trouble.

Edward went onto the attack, uniting the feuding barons in the fight against England's enemies. Luckily he'd inherited his grandfather's military skill. He defeated the Scots at Halidon Hill in 1333. Two years later his army defeated them again at Neville's Cross.

The French Connection

Edward certainly didn't lack for cheek. Soon he was claiming the French throne as well. He based his claim on inheritance through his mother, who was the sister of Charles IV of France who had died in 1328. The French didn't recognise inheritance through the female line. Instead they crowned Charles's nearest male heir, his cousin, who became Philip VI.

Edward set off for France to defend his claim, beginning what was to be called the Hundred Years War. In 1340 he defeated the French in a sea-battle at Sluys.

Further victories followed at Crecy in 1346 and Poitiers in 1356, where English archers polished off the French knights at long range with their deadly longbows.

(The French considered this particularly unsporting. After all, the archers were only peasants - and wars were supposed to be won by gentlemen.)

The Black Prince

Hero of these later battles was Edward's eldest son, yet another Edward, who became known as the Black Prince from the colour of his armour.

For a time everything seemed to go well for Edward III. It all seemed too good to last, and, of course, it was.

The Black Death

In 1348 the plague known as the Black Death struck northern Europe. England's population was actually halved and her military strength greatly weakened.

Queen Philippa died in 1369, and it was around this time that Edward's luck really turned against him. Even the war in France was going badly. Before long England was barely managing to cling on to a handful of French coastal towns.

A Sad Decline

As time went by, the aging king began to lose his grip on the barons and on an increasingly-rebellious Parliament.

He acquired a mistress called Alice Perrers, described by a historian of the time as 'a wanton baggage'. Greedy and rapacious she made the king's later years a misery. She and her daughter Isabella were said to sleep with the King together, and it seems likely that they infected him with venereal disease.

Edward's pride and joy, the Black Prince was never to become king. He became ill when fighting in Spain and died in 1376.

The king fell ill and died in 1377.

(Alice pinched the royal jewellery from his body, and retired to live in comfort on the proceeds.)

Fifty Years a King

Edward III reigned for an astonishing fifty years. As a young man he was tall and handsome with red-gold hair. Popular with barons and common people alike, for much of his long reign he was successful in battle abroad, and a good administrator at home. He was happily married to Queen Philippa for over forty years, and he had a son, the Black Prince, whose exploits matched his own. Despite the sad, not to say sordid, ending of his life, Edward III remains one of England's greatest kings.

RICHARD II - 1377-1399

Because the Black Prince had died a year before his father, the crown passed to his son Richard, a boy of ten. The poor lad was so exhausted by the lengthy coronation ceremonies that he fell fast asleep and had to be carried from the Abbey to Westminster Hall.

RICHARD II, AGED TEN, PRACTISES
SLEEPING WHILE SITTING

A Brave Boy King

Since the King was so young, England was ruled for ten years by royal advisers. In 1381 they decided to impose a bob-a-nob Poll Tax - a shilling a head on everyone over fifteen. This led to an immediate Peasants' Revolt.

(Proof that Maggie Thatcher can't have studied history - or she'd never have tried it on again.)

The revolt was quelled by an act of great personal bravery from young King Richard, who was still only fourteen. He rode out to meet the rebellious mob at Smithfield and succeeded in calming them. It was to be the high point of his reign.

Love and Death

In 1382 Richard married Anne of Bohemia, with whom he had fallen madly in love. Their marriage was a genuine love-match - one of the very few in history.

In 1389 Richard formally took over the government of the country and at first he ruled wisely and well. However, he had come to the throne in exceptionally difficult times. The Black Death was still raging and the country was in a troubled state with rebellion rumbling under the surface.

When Queen Anne died in 1394, most probably from the plague, Richard became crazed with grief, completely destroying the palace in which she'd lived.

From this time his character seemed to change. He became gloomy and melancholic, with a fierce determination to rule unopposed.

The feeling is expressed in Shakespeare's play:
'Not all the water in the rough rude sea
Can wash the balm off from an anointed king
The breath of worldly men cannot depose
The deputy elected by the Lord.'

Like other mistaken monarchs, Richard felt simply *being* a king was enough. It wasn't, and never has been. Thrones may be inherited, but to keep them they have to be earned.

(Present-day royals please note!)

Bolingbroke's Challenge

Happy as it was, Richard's marriage to Anne had been childless. The powerful families of Lancaster, York and Gloucester all had their eyes on the throne.

The threatened Richard made the mistake of trying to put the clock back, trying to tyrannise over nobles and parliament alike. In 1397 he exiled his powerful cousin Henry Bolingbroke, later seizing his lands. Inevitably this led to revolt. In 1399 Henry Bolingbroke returned to claim his inheritance. The barons rallied to Henry and Richard was defeated and deposed.

Henry Bolingbroke, Duke of Lancaster, became King Henry IV.

A Sad End

Imprisoned in Pontefract Castle, Richard sunk deeper into melancholy, refusing to eat. According to King Henry, Richard virtually starved himself to death, dying in 1400.

Naturally enough, there were rumours that Richard had been murdered. To disprove them, King Henry brought Richard's body to London and paraded it through the streets. Richard was buried beside his beloved Anne in Westminster Abbey.

It was a sad end to an unhappy reign. Richard's mistake had been in trying to rule as an 'absolute monarch' - a ruler with virtually unlimited powers, like the kings of France and Spain. But the

country had progressed far beyond this by now. The barons were far too powerful, and just wouldn't put up with it.

As far as the British were concerned, the days of absolute monarchy were gone for good.

(Shakespearean note: if the current collection of kings is starting to sound familiar, it's probably because you've come across them in the works of our greatest dramatist, William Shakespeare. Will wrote no fewer than ten historical plays, including, of course, 'Richard II'.

THE PLANTAGENETS
The House of Lancaster

HENRY IV - 1399-1413

Bolingbroke became king in uneasy circumstances. Grabbing the throne when the current king died without an heir was one thing. Shoving a legitimate, if unsatisfactory, king off the throne while he was still alive was something else.

Since he was the son of the fourth son of Edward III, Henry had a fairly reasonable claim to the crown. (Edward Mortimer, son of Edward III's *third* son, had an even better one. But Edward was only eight years old. In these turbulent times, barons and Parliament alike wanted a strong, and grown-up, ruler.)

All the same, Henry knew he had only become king because the country got fed up with Richard. What would happen if they got tired of Henry too? Will Shakespeare summed it up:

'Uneasy lies the head that wears a crown.'

A Fighting King

Short, stout and stubborn, with little of the late Richard's charm, Henry IV had a tough time as king. He spent most of his reign simply fighting for survival.

The Scots attacked again, making more trouble in the north. The once-defeated Welsh made a comeback, producing a warrior prince called Owen Glendower - or if you're Welsh, Glyndwr - who mounted a guerilla-style rebellion that took Henry ten years to put down. Owen was aided by the ever-helpful French who sent soldiers to support him. When they weren't helping the Welsh, the French were happily attacking the south coast of England.

Rebellious Barons

In addition to trouble abroad, Henry had enemies at home.

Two powerful families, the Percys and the Mortimers, kept

mounting rebellions against him. The Archbishop of York kept on encouraging the rebels. Henry lost patience and executed him, shocking the common people and incurring the anger of the Church.

(When Henry developed an unpleasant skin disease, people said God was punishing him for giving the archbishop the chop.)

Somehow Henry survived, fighting on all fronts. In 1380 he married Lady Mary de Bohun who gave him five sons and two daughters. The eldest son died young, and it was the second, another Henry, who succeeded his father.

When he wasn't at war, Henry was wrangling with Parliament, trying to raise enough taxes to keep on fighting his enemies.

Death in Jerusalem

According to an old prophecy, Henry IV was destined to die in Jerusalem. He probably thought as long as he kept clear of the Holy Land he'd be okay. When he collapsed at his prayers in Westminster Abbey, he was carried to a room called the Jerusalem Chamber - and there he died, worn out in 1422.

Henry IV had grabbed hold of the throne by force. Amazingly, he'd managed to hang on to to it, but sometimes he must have wondered if it was worth it...

(Shakespeare covers his reign in two history plays called, believe it or not, 'Henry IV Part One' and 'Henry IV Part Two'.)

HENRY V - 1413-1422

Henry IV's reign had been a holding operation. This new branch of the Plantagenets needed a solid success to consolidate their grip on the throne. In Henry V that's exactly what they got. Handsome and athletic, a good scholar, a fine musician and a superb soldier, Henry V was a superstar from the start.

Superstar Henry

(We all know the story from Shakespeare - the playboy Prince changes his character when he becomes king, casting off former friends and boozing companions like the fat knight Falstaff. Shakespeare depicts young Henry as a cool, calculating type, cunning and manipulative beneath a cheerful, friendly exterior.)

Henry V is undoubtedly the greatest of England's warrior kings. He started his soldiering in Wales, helping his father to fight Owen Glendower. When he became king he cunningly distracted his rebellious barons from attacking each other - and him - by putting new life into that ever-popular old favourite the long- running war with France. A war at which, you'll remember, England hadn't been doing too well lately.

HENRY V REALLY WANTED A
'WEDGE' HAIRCUT, BUT THE
ROYAL BARBER FAILED TO
GET IT QUITE RIGHT

Henry Victorious

Taking an invading army to France, Henry scored a brilliant victory at Agincourt in 1415 - helped by those still-deadly English archers. In Shakespeare's 'Henry', the story produces some of his most inspiring speeches:

'Once more unto the breach dear friends, once more
Or close the wall up with our English dead!'
and:
'Follow your spirit and upon this charge
Cry, 'God for Harry! England and St George!'
And most famous of all:
'We few, we happy few, we band of brothers;
For he today that sheds his blood with me
Shall be my brother...
And gentlemen in England now a-bed
Shall think themselves accurs'd they were not here
And hold their manhoods cheap whiles any speak
That fought with us upon St Crispin's day.'

(You can see it all in two films of 'Henry V', first with the late Lord Olivier, more recently in young Ken Branagh's version.)

By 1419 English armies had reached the walls of Paris. Fed up with being bashed by the apparently invincible English - not to mention being made to look like armoured porcupines by their archers - the French gave a Gallic shrug and decided to give up.

HENRY V LOVED MUSIC — AT THE AG
TEN HE OWNED A HARP

Treaty Time

The Treaty of Troyes, signed in 1420, recognised Henry V of England as regent of France and official heir to the French throne. This was a bit of a blow for the Dauphin, the French king's son, who'd naturally assumed the job was his. To seal the bargain Henry was given the hand in marriage of Catherine de Valois,daughter of Charles VI, the mad King of France.

Henry Rules, OK!

King of England, future King of France, Henry V was top monarch, the most powerful man in Europe. Having settled the French, he decided to sort out the Saracens. His ambition, like that of most medieval monarchs, was to re-conquer the Holy Land and restore Jerusalem to Christendom.

He might even have done it, but fate intervened. While mopping up a few remaining Frogs, Henry V went down with a sudden attack of dysentery, dying at Bois de Vincennes in 1422.

He was thirty-five years old and his short but glorious reign had lasted for just nine years.

X-RAY THROUGH HAT SHOWING STATE OF HAIR

NO-ONE UNDERSTOOD HAIRDRESSING IN THE TIME OF HENRY V, SO THEY WORE ELABORATE HATS TO COVER UP THE MESS THEIR HAIR WAS IN

HENRY VI - 1422-1461 AND 1470-1471

After a short, successful reign there comes, you've guessed it, a long disastrous one - or rather two. Henry VI is one of two English kings to have reigned twice. He's also the youngest king to have gained the throne - he inherited the crown when he was only eight months old.

The Baby King

Henry VI was born in 1421. Soon afterwards his mother, Catherine de Valois, found herself a widow at twenty, after a year and a half of marriage. She travelled back to England with Henry's body, and was given Baynard's Castle as her residence. (She hadn't been installed very long when there were scandalous rumours about her friendship with a handsome young Welshman called Owen Tudor. There were

HENRY VI BECAME KING OF ENGLAND AT THE AGE OF NINE MONTHS AND KING OF FRANCE BY THE AGE OF EIGHT.

A PRETTY COOL KID.

rumours of a secret marriage and they certainly had three children. More of this later.)

The baby king attended Parliament in his mother's lap. He was crowned King of England when he was eight years old, and King of France on the death of his grandfather, Charles VI of France.

Since the king was still a child, the Duke of Bedford became Regent of France, and the Duke of Gloucester Regent of England.

Trouble in France

With the death of Henry V, France started slipping from England's grasp again. A divinely-inspired peasant girl called Joan of Arc was inspiring the French to fight. The English burned her as a witch in 1431 but her spirit lived on and the French resistance to English rule grew steadily stronger. Normandy was lost in 1450, Gascony in 1451. By 1453 the English had been chased out of France - the Hundred Years War was over.

Henry the Good

Henry grew up to be a simple, almost saintly king, with an un-medieval distaste for violence and cruelty. He hated passing death sentences, and pardoned rebels whenever he could. Keen on education, he founded Eton, and King's College, Cambridge.

All these good qualities, of course, made poor Henry quite unsuited to be a medieval monarch - the job really needed a tough, ruthless warrior like his dad. Unfortunately, Henry also took after his mad French grandfather, suffering occasional bouts of mental instability.

Henry Cracks Up

Henry took over the rule of England in 1437. In 1445 he married Margaret of Anjou, a tough and determined lady with all the strength and determination her husband lacked. After eight years of marriage they had a son. Soon after that Henry suffered the first of his mental breakdowns and Richard, Duke of York ruled as Protector.

Lancaster v. York

The Plantagenet family tree had two powerful branches, the House of Lancaster, currently providing the kings, and the House of York. The Yorkists thought it was time they had a turn, especially since Henry wasn't doing too well. In 1455 this family quarrel developed into a full-scale civil war. It was called the War of the Roses - Lancastrians wore the Red Rose of Lancaster, Yorkists the White Rose of York.

THE WARS OF THE ROSES

Henry Deposed

In 1460 Henry was defeated at Northampton, and forced to accept the Duke of York as his heir, cutting out his own son.

The queen, however, rallied the king's Lancastrian forces and managed to rescue him, after a battle in which Richard of York was killed.

Edward, the new Duke of York (confused? You will be - it gets worse!) defeated the Lancastrians in battle at Towton, and Henry fled to Scotland. The Duke of York declared Henry to be deposed, and had himself crowned King Edward IV. (Pay attention - this is where it gets really complicated!)

Henry Restored

In 1464 Henry, now ex-king, came down from Scotland and led an uprising in an attempt to get his throne back. The rising failed and Henry was tossed into the Tower of London.

The queen, however, still hadn't given up. She left Scotland for France, taking her son Edward with her, and appealed for help to her cousin Louis XI. She returned to England with a French army, got beaten at Hexham and chased back to France.

After seven years in exile she tried again, forming an alliance with the Earl of Warwick, known as the Kingmaker, an old ally of Edward's who'd decided to change sides.

This time the attempt was successful. When Warwick's army landed Edward IV fled to Holland. In 1470 Henry, now no more than a puppet-king, was taken out of the Tower and became king again - but not for long.

Deposed Again

In 1471 Edward returned to claim his throne, defeating Warwick and the queen's Lancastrian forces at Tewkesbury. Henry's son and heir, who was also called Edward, was murdered soon after the battle.

Henry, deposed again, was returned to the Tower. His death was announced just a few weeks later. He's believed to have been stabbed to death by the restored King Edward's brother, Richard Duke of Gloucester, who was later to become - wait for it - King Richard III... (All clear so far? Well, I warned you...)

Henry VI's story is one of the saddest in all our Royal history. A simple, kindly man, handicapped by recurrent mental illness, he just didn't have what it took to survive in the jungle of medieval politics.

Margaret's Fate

And what about Margaret, the tough and loyal queen who had fought so hard for her poor, weak husband's throne?

She was captured as well, and sent to the Tower. It's said that she arrived on the night her husband was murdered, and saw his dead body being carried past her window...

She must have been pretty certain she was next.

However, she herself escaped the same fate, partly because of her powerful relatives, partly because of her considerable cash value. The restored Edward IV demanded a ransom of 50,000 crowns for her release. Margaret's devoted father, a minor monarch called King Rene, King of Naples and Sicily and Count of Anjou, managed to raise the loot by selling his possessions in Provence to Louis XI.

In 1475 Margaret was finally released. She eventually joined her father in his country retreat near Angers in France. After all the murderous excitement of life with English royalty she was probably glad of the peace and quiet...

THE PLANTAGENETS
The House of York

EDWARD IV - 1461-1470 AND 1471-1483

So now another branch of the feuding Plantagenet family had managed to get their hands on the crown.

We've already seen something of Edward's stormy career. Avenging his dead father, he managed to seize the throne for himself. Edward was a forceful, buccaneering type, a good soldier and a capable administrator.

A Romantic King

Edward was said to be something of a ladies' man and he certainly had his romantic side. He fell madly in love with a beautiful widow, Elizabeth, Lady Grey. Virtuous as well as beautiful, she refused to become his mistress, saying if she wasn't good enough to be his queen she was too good to be his harlot. Edward gave in - he married her.

Secret Marriage

At first the marriage was kept secret. But later on, when Parliament urged him to marry some suitable foreign princess, Edward calmly announced that he was married already. Defiantly he brought Elizabeth to London and had her crowned as his queen.

Family Problems

He also honoured her family, the Woodvilles, making her father an Earl and creating him Lord High Constable of England. This caused quite a scandal. The Woodvilles had been Lancastrians - the other side in the Wars of the Roses.

Edward's brother, Richard, Duke of Gloucester, was particularly put out, and made no secret of his dislike for his new sister-in-law.

Despite these family problems, it seems to have been a happy marriage. There were ten children, three sons and seven daughters.

Setback

Edward suffered a brief career setback in 1470 when his old mate the Earl of Warwick switched sides and chased him from the throne. Edward had to make a rapid retreat to France, leaving his wife and family to take refuge in the Sanctuary at Westminster.

A year later Edward was back in power and the men who'd displaced him were dead.

George in the Drink

Edward certainly didn't lack for ruthlessness. His own brother, George, Duke of Clarence, had sided with the Earl of Warwick during the temporary restoration of Henry VI.

George was arrested as a traitor and thrown in the Tower of London. Like so many others he never came out again. He is said to have been drowned in a barrel of Malmsey wine.

(Well, I suppose if you've got to go...)

GEORGE, DUKE OF CLARENCE, DROWNED IN A BARREL OF MALMSEY WINE

A Competent King

Edward himself went quite suddenly, dying of pneumonia in 1483, just before his forty-first birthday. Despite the unscrupulous way he'd got hold of and held on to the throne, he proved a surprisingly good king once he was in power, a hard worker and an efficient administrator. Tall and handsome, apparently easy-going, he was a shrewd politician. It was said he knew the name of every important person in the kingdom - and how much money they had as well.

Edward IV was very much a man of his time, competent, determined and ruthless - and quite prepared to dispose of anyone who stood in his way.

EDWARD V - 1483

When her husband died, the queen took refuge in Sanctuary at Westminster - again - with her children, fearing the enmity of her sinister brother-in-law, Richard of Gloucester.

Her eldest son, Edward, now (in name at least) King Edward V, had already been taken to the Tower of London. The queen was persuaded to allow his brother Richard to join him. A few months later, both boys had disappeared. They were never seen again.

The Missing Princes

These two children are the famous Princes in the Tower. It has long been believed they were both murdered, smothered in their sleep on the orders of Richard of Gloucester, simply because they stood between him and the throne. The skeletons of two children were found in the White Tower in 1674.

RICHARD III - 1483-1485

Now we come to one of royal history's greatest villains, a man who makes Bad King John look like a choir-boy.

As he says in Shakespeare's play:

'I am determined to prove a villain,
And hate the idle pleasures of these days.'
    In Shakespeare's play of the same name, Richard is depicted as a sinister hunchback with a strange, almost hypnotic charm, especially for the opposite sex.
'Teach not thy lip such scorn, for it was made
For kissing, lady, not for such contempt',
he tells the woman he is wooing at her husband's funeral.

The Wicked Uncle

    As Duke of Gloucester, Richard had already been mixed up in the sudden and suspicious deaths of his brother's predecessor, King Henry VI, and his own other brother, George, Duke of Clarence. (The one who died, presumably happy, drowning in wine.)

    On the death of Edward IV, Richard became Lord High Protector of England. Richard's young nephew, the new King Edward V, was escorted to London by another uncle, Earl Rivers, and his half-brother, Lord Grey.

THE LITTLE PRINCES GET THE WRONG IDEA

Richard met the party in force and hijacked the new king, ceremonially presenting him to the good citizens of London as their new ruler. Kindly Uncle Richard, of course, was simply the king's loyal protector - and we know how long that lasted.

Ruthless Richard

Alarmed at Richard's growing power, some of the Council, led by Lord Hastings, made plans to get the young King away from him.Richard arrested the plotters and beheaded them without trial. To be on the safe side he executed Earl Rivers, the new king's uncle, and Lord Grey as well.

That left the young king and his brother, those two unfortunate Princes in the Tower - and, as we've seen, *they* weren't a problem for very long...

To make doubly sure, Richard dropped a word in the ear of a friendly cleric, who preached a sermon saying Edward IV's marriage had been invalid, so his children were all bastards.

Richard Triumphant

By now Parliament had got the message - opposing Richard was an unhealthy occupation. Since there were no other suitable candidates still alive (funny, that!) they took the hint and offered him the crown. In 1483, tricky Richard was crowned King.

Given the violent way Richard III had got his bloody hands on the crown, it's scarcely surprising that he didn't hold on to it for very long.

Henry Tudor's Rebellion

The Plantagenet family was divided into Lancastrians and Yorkists, remember - and Richard was a Yorkist. Before long the Lancastrians were mounting a challenge. They were led by a certain Henry Tudor, whose claim to the throne was, if anything, even shakier than Richard's own.

In 1485 Richard III led his troops to meet the new challenger at the battle of Bosworth Field. He must have been feeling pretty confident. He started the battle with his army outnumbering Henry's ten to one - but Richard had never really mastered the art of being popular. Halfway through the battle most of his army changed sides, and suddenly everything was lost.

Richard's Defeat

'A horse, a horse, my kingdom for a horse!' cried Richard - but it was too late. As brave as he was villainous, Richard fought till the last. When he was killed the crown was hacked from his head, and rolled under a bush. Soon afterwards someone found it - and placed it upon the head of Henry Tudor.

It was a short but amazingly bloodstained career. Richard III died at the age of thirty-two, after being king for a mere two years. Maybe crime doesn't pay after all...

A Misjudged King?

Now it's only fair to Richard III's ghost to tell you that *some* historians say much of the above is a pack of lies.

Richard, they say, was stitched up rotten by Tudor historians who came after his time. Their aim was to blacken Richard III's name in order to whitewash the upstart Tudors who followed him. Shakespeare followed the official party line in his play - it wasn't safe to do anything else. And besides, it was such a good story...

The Real Story?

So what's the real truth? For a start, say these historians, Richard wasn't even a hunchback. He just had one shoulder higher than the other. And there's no real proof he murdered the Princes in the Tower. There's even a story the Princes were seen alive *after* Bosworth - which means that if anyone polished them off, it was probably the incoming Tudors.

(Historical detective story note: the crime novelist Josephine Tey was so impressed by these theories that she wrote a book called 'The Daughter of Time'. Her convalescing detective hero proves Richard III's innocence by conducting historical research from his hospital bed!)

It's all too long ago to be really sure.

Meanwhile Shakespeare's genius has done its work. Most people will always see King Richard III scuttling about his court like a great black spider, seducing the widow of one of his victims over her husband's coffin and happily planning the next round of executions...

RICHARD III

THE HOUSE OF TUDOR

THE HOUSE OF TUDOR

HENRY VII - 1485-1509

Henry VII's claim to the throne follows a rather roundabout route. Remember the handsome young Welsh squire who had a fling with, and perhaps secretly married, Henry V's widow, Catherine de Valois? That was Henry's grandfather.

His father, Edmund Tudor, Earl of Richmond, married Margaret Beaufort, only child of the Duke of Somerset, who was descended from John of Gaunt who was the third son of Edward III - oh, never mind. The point is, his claim was pretty feeble.

Henry also had a rather comical claim to royalty on the male side. His grandad, Owen Tudor, claimed to be descended from Coel Hen Godeborg, a king from way back in Roman times, better known as Old King Cole! Henry could also claim descent from the great Welsh hero Owen Glendower.

Henry and the Pretenders

But in those days it wasn't so much the strength of your claim as the size of your army that counted. Henry had achieved a decisive victory at the battle of Bosworth and the crown was his. He consolidated his newly-royal position by marrying Elizabeth, daughter of Edward IV, and settled down to reign.

There were still plenty of problems.

Henry VII was particularly plagued with pretenders - fake noblemen who claimed to have right to the throne. Both pretenders had very silly names - maybe that's why they wanted to change them.

The first was Lambert Simnel who pretended to be Edward, Earl of Warwick, son of George, Duke of Clarence. (You remember poor old George, the one who literally died of drink, drowned in a wine barrel?)

King Lambert

Lambert managed to drum up some support in Ireland - they like a good laugh over there. Besides, it was a good chance to stir up a bit of trouble for the Brits. He actually got himself crowned Edward VI in Dublin in 1487. Taking the whole thing far too seriously he immediately invaded England and got soundly defeated and captured by Henry at Stoke-on-Trent.

Henry, who wasn't without a sense of humour himself, pardoned the lad and gave him a job as a turnspit in the royal kitchens - one of the earliest examples of a youth employment scheme.

HENRY VII DISAPPROVED OF SILLY
GAMES OF "LET'S PRETEND."

Pretender Perkin

The next pretender didn't come out of things so well. He was called Perkin Warbeck and he claimed to be Richard, Duke of York, younger son of Edward IV. Not only did he find support in Europe, he managed to con not only the Irish but the Scots. He was accepted as King Richard IV of England at the Scottish court, and allowed to marry a Scottish noblewoman as well.

Cutting short the honeymoon, Perkin cunningly invaded England by way of Cornwall. He only got as far as Exeter before being defeated and captured by King Henry.

Either the joke was wearing thin by now or King Henry had enough spit-turners - he tossed poor Perkin into the Tower of London. There Perkin confessed his imposture, and later made the mistake of trying to escape. He was re-captured and hanged.

A Careful King

Henry VII proved to be just what the country needed, a quiet, careful king who provided some much-needed stability after all the recent upsets. He followed a cautious foreign policy and gave some much- needed encouragement to trade.

The inevitable rebels were dealt with firmly but without excessive

THE LION AND THE UNICORN GET ON
FAMOUSLY DURING THE REIGN OF HENRY VII

bloodshed. (There had been so many battles, rebellions and executions recently that the nobility was running seriously short of manpower.)

Although he had the reputation of being tight with money, Henry VII kept a respectable court and forked up handsomely to build the palaces of Richmond and Greenwich.

He added a beautiful chapel, which bears his name, to Westminster Abbey, and it's there he lies buried.

HENRY VIII - 1509-1547

Henry VIII is another king with a serious image problem.

This time it's a film - 'The Private Life of Henry VIII'. It was made by Alexander Korda back in the thirties but it still crops up on TV. The film shows Henry as an incredible fatty - played by a real-life fatty, the late, great Charles Laughton - chewing whole chickens and chucking the bones over his shoulder. (More recently there was a very popular BBC Classic Serial, 'The Six Wives of Henry VIII' - but it's that old movie that everyone remembers.)

Henry's Half-dozen

The other thing people remember about Henry VIII is his many marriages. A lot of people have a vague idea that Henry VIII had eight wives and chopped off *all* their heads. In fact he was married six times, and he only executed two of them. Quite restrained really, ask any married man.

Handsome Henry

It comes as something of a shock to realise that Henry VIII started life as a slim young prince. He was eighteen when he inherited the throne, tall, fair and handsome, a good dancer and a keen sportsman. He spoke several languages, played a number of musical instruments and composed music - he's said to have composed the traditional tune 'Greenleeves', which you still hear today.

Wife No 1

Besides all the usual problems of kingship, Henry had that old obsession of all monarchs, the need for a son and heir to inherit his throne. Wasting no time, he got married in 1509, the year he came to the throne. The bride was Catherine of Aragon. She was the daughter of the King of Spain and the widow of Henry's elder brother Arthur, who'd died before he could become king. The event was marked with lots of feasting, jousting and Royal processions, establishing the fun-loving image of 'Bluff King Hal'.

Fighting the French

Like all good English kings, Henry turned his attention to fighting the French. He invaded France and scored a victory at the Battle of the Spurs.

Settling the Scots

Back home, the Scots had the cheek to invade England. Henry's army defeated them soundly at Flodden Field. James IV, King of Scotland, was killed in the battle.

Where's the Heir?

So far so good. But things weren't going so well in the son-and-heir stakes. Poor Catherine of Aragon eventually bore Henry six children. Sadly they were all sickly. Only one of them survived - and she was a girl.

Henry decided the only thing to do was to get rid of Catherine and marry his mistress, a sexy young lady-in-waiting called Anne Boleyn. She was dead keen to be queen - and she was already pregnant.

Royal Divorce

Henry ordered his Chancellor, Cardinal Wolsey, to arrange a divorce on the grounds that Henry should never have married his brother's widow in the first place. Catherine and her powerful relatives opposed the divorce like mad. The Pope wasn't too keen either, and Wolsey failed.

The Church of England

Not a man to put up with opposition, Henry broke off relations with Rome, declaring himself Supreme Head of the English Church. (It's a position English monarchs still hold today. It's the reason a bishop recently declared that poor old Charles wasn't fit to be king - and therefore Head of the Church - because of his alleged extra-marital carrying-on. Henry would have given him the chop for his cheek.)

Cranmer Comes Through

Having shown the Pope he wouldn't stand any nonsense, and incidentally founding the Church of England in the process, Henry made Thomas Cranmer Archbishop of Canterbury. Cranmer, surprise surprise, duly declared Henry's marriage to Catherine null and void. In 1533 Henry married Anne Boleyn. With suspicious speed she bore him a child - a daughter. Foiled again!

(But what a daughter! Christened Elizabeth, the baby grew up to be a tough and stubborn redhead - who survived to become one of England's greatest queens.)

Exit Wolsey

Poor old Wolsey was accused of high treason because of his failure to get Henry his divorce.

In his play 'Henry VIII' Shakespeare has him say sadly:
'Had I but serv'd my God with half the zeal
I serv'd my king he would not in mine age
Have left me naked to mine enemies.'

Wolsey escaped the axe, but only by dying before his trial.
Henry replaced him with an old friend, Sir Thomas More. But More's conscience wouldn't allow him to accept Henry as head of the

Church, so Henry executed him.

(The sad story is movingly told in 'A Man for All Seasons', a stage play (and later a film) by Robert Bolt.)

Death of Catherine

In 1536 the divorced Catherine of Aragon died. Henry was so upset that he ordered himself a new yellow outfit, a thanksgiving mass and a feast, followed by dancing.

Goodbye Anne Boleyn

Since Anne Boleyn had failed to come up with the goods, Henry decided she'd have to go. Unable to come up with any really solid evidence, he arrested her on trumped-up charges of being a witch - she had six fingers on her left hand. To be on the safe side he also accused her of incest with her own brother and had her executed on Tower Green. He executed the brother as well.

SHALL I BEHEAD THE ROYAL EGG, SIRE ?

Number Three

Henry's third wife was Jane Seymour, one of Anne's ladies-in-waiting, with whom he'd been having an affair - she'd evidently got tired of waiting! Jane Seymour eventually produced the long-awaited male heir, but she died soon afterwards.

Enter Anne of Cleves

Before long Henry was looking around for wife number four. Eventually he fixed upon a foreign princess called Anne of Cleves. Since he'd never actually seen her, and Polaroids hadn't been invented, he despatched the court painter Holbein to knock up a quick portrait. Henry liked the picture, the marriage was duly arranged, and Anne set off for England. When Henry met her in the flesh he was severely disappointed. He said Holbein's picture had been far too flattering and Anne was 'nothing so well' as he'd been told, referring to her unkindly as 'The Flanders mare'.

ANNE OF CLEVES

Divorced Again

It was too late to get out of the marriage, but Anne and Henry spent their wedding night playing cards. Six months later, he had the marriage annulled. Anne agreed without fuss, and Henry gave her a palace and a handsome income. He actually became very fond of her after the divorce, calling her his beloved sister, and paying her frequent visits.

HENRY VIII DISCUSSES WIVES WITH A FRIEND

Sex-kitten Catherine

Since Anne of Cleves had been on the dull side, Henry looked out for something livelier - and he certainly found it.

Catherine Howard seems to have been a real sex-kitten. She was young, she was lovely and she was decidedly hot stuff. By the time Henry met her, she'd had already had several steamy affairs, with her music teacher, with Francis Dereham, a family retainer, and with her cousin Thomas Culpepper.

Henry fell for her on sight and they were married a few weeks after the divorce. All this happened in 1540 - Henry had been married, divorced and re-married all in the same year.

Catherine Gets Careless

For a while things went well. Henry was nearly fifty by now. He'd lost the good looks of his youth and he was overweight and ill. But marriage to a beautiful young wife revived him, at least for a time. There were more feasts and royal tours, and he showered his new wife with gifts, including jewellery and land.

Catherine, however, was a lot less keen on Henry than he was on her. She soon tired of her fat old husband and returned to her former lovers, Dereham and Culpepper.

Henry was unsuspecting at first, and Catherine became careless. During a royal trip North, one of her ladies-in-waiting, Lady Rochford, smuggled Culpepper into the Queen's quarters whenever she got the chance.

A Shock for Henry

An informer told Archbishop Cranmer, and Cranmer told the King. Henry was heartbroken at first, refusing to believe him. When convinced that the story was true he flew into a jealous rage, sending Catherine and her accomplice Lady Rochford to the executioners block. The lovers, Dereham and Culpepper, were executed as well. (Get involved in royal shenanigans in those days and you risked a lot more than exposure in the tabloids.)

One Last Wife

Now old and weary and ill, Henry had given up any hope of more heirs. Nevertheless, in 1543 he married again. Catherine Parr, his sixth and last wife, was to be a combined nurse and companion for the ageing King, and a mother to his surviving children, Mary, Elizabeth and Edward.

(He certainly didn't choose her for her looks - Catherine was unkindly described as being even plainer than Anne of Cleves.)

Already twice-widowed, she was a sensible, kindly woman, and something of an intellectual. When Henry went to the wars for the last time in 1544 he left Catherine as Governor of the Realm.

Henry's sixth and last marriage seems to have been his happiest, and he and Catherine were still together when he died in 1547. She was the only one of Henry's wives to outlive him - quite an achievement in itself.

MEN WERE VAIN ABOUT THEIR LEGS AND TOOK EXTREME MEASURES TO HAVE THEM MADE LONGER.

A Contradictory King

Henry VIII's astonishing marital record has overshadowed the rest of his reign. In some ways he is the most contradictory of kings. Popular and energetic in his youth, he became oppressive and tyrannical in his old age.

He was a cunning and careful king, well able to look after himself. If a nobleman looked like getting too powerful, Henry - and most of his court - would go and stay with him for a while. By the end of an expensive royal visit, the poor nobleman was too broke to get up to mischief.

He pursued an aggressive foreign policy - and nearly bankrupted the country with pointless military adventures. The power of Parliament grew in Henry's reign. The king had to summon them often, to raise the money he needed for foreign wars.

Henry VIII broke away from the Church of Rome, establishing the Church of England with himself at its head. He ordered the Dissolution of the Monasteries - mainly so he could seize the wealth of the Church.

For all his faults, and there were many of them, Henry VIII is the most memorable of English kings.

As the old music-hall song goes: 'I'm 'Enery the Eighth I am!' No-one will ever forget it.

EDWARD VI - 1547-1553

Henry VIII had broken with Rome, shattered the old medieval order and set up the Church of England, in a frantic quest for just one thing - a son to inherit the throne. Thanks to his third wife, Jane Seymour, he'd managed it, even though she died soon after the much-wanted heir was born.

Weedy Edward

Edward VI hardly seems worth all the fuss. He grew up to be a pale and scholarly youth, quite unlike his lusty, outrageous father. He studied Greek, Latin and French and relaxed by playing the lute and studying the stars. He was educated as a strict Protestant, and took a keen interest in the new, non-Catholic religion, influenced by John Knox, Ridley, Latimer and Cranmer, all keen religious reformers.

Unlucky Uncles

Edward came to the throne as a boy of ten. Naturally the real ruling was done by others, all struggling to seize power. The most successful, at least to begin with, was Edward's maternal uncle, Lord Hertford, who became Duke of Somerset, Protector of the Realm.

Another uncle, Thomas Seymour, was less fortunate. He was accused of treason by jealous rivals. Although the lively and charming Tom Seymour had always been his favourite uncle, Edward was forced to agree to his execution.

A few years later Protector Somerset was accused and executed in turn. He was replaced by John Dudley, Earl of Warwick, who became Duke of Northumberland.

The End of Edward

Always a sickly child, Edward VI fell ill and died when he was still only fifteen. Some historians think he was educated to death - a warning to us all. A more likely theory is that over-zealous court physicians, always worried about the poor lad's health, actually dosed him to death with the dubious medicines of the day. Whatever the cause, Edward died after a short six-year reign, and was buried in Westminster Abbey.

MARY I - 1553-1558

When Edward died, his Protector, the Duke of Northumberland, attempted to consolidate his power by proclaiming Lady Jane Grey, granddaughter of Henry VIII's sister Mary, as queen. He cunningly married her off to his sixteen-year-old son, Lord Guildford of Dudley. But the English didn't want Lady Jane as their queen. Most people thought Mary, daughter of Henry VIII and Catherine of Aragon, had a far better claim.

LADY JANE GREY

A Catholic Queen

Accompanied by her half-sister Elizabeth, Mary set off for London where the barons rallied round her. Lady Jane and her husband, pawns in the hands of their ambitious relative, were arrested and executed, as was Northumberland himself.

Mary was proclaimed queen in 1553, and promptly started trying to put the religious clock back. Like the late Edward she was a rather sickly, scholarly type, with a keen interest in religion. But in her case it was the Catholic religion, her mother's religion, from which Henry VIII had broken away.

During Edward's time she'd been put under pressure to become Protestant. When she came to the throne, she saw it as her duty to restore the Catholic religion. She also announced her decision to marry one of the Continent's leading Catholic royals, Philip of Spain.

Protestant Rebellion

The newly-Protestant English didn't care for being told to become Catholic again, and they liked the idea of a foreign monarch even less. Rebellion broke out in Kent but it was ruthlessly suppressed, and its leader, Sir Thomas Wyatt, was, you've guessed it, executed. (Beheading was *the* growth industry in those days.)

The marriage went ahead as planned in 1554. Mary insisted that Philip be given the title of king, which makes him England's only King Consort.

Philip Goes Home

Their marriage, like so many other royal marriages, wasn't a great success. Mary was madly in love with Philip, but the feeling was far from mutual. He disliked her looks, complained about her smell, and took himself back to Spain in 1555.

Mary's only consolation was her belief that she was pregnant, but even that turned out to be a false alarm. She was never to produce a royal heir - not surprisingly, since her husband was in Spain for most of their marriage.

Bloody Mary

Disappointed and rejected, Mary turned her attention to persecuting the Protestants. Like her husband Philip, who was doing the same thing back in Spain, she favoured the old-fashioned methods. Protestant bishops like Ridley, Latimer and Cranley were burnt at the stake, and hundreds more Protestants lost their lives. Because of all this slaughter Mary was nicknamed 'Bloody Mary'. This makes her the only English monarch to give her name to a cocktail - a blood-coloured vodka-and-tomato juice mixture.

Philip's Return

In 1557 Philip made a brief reappearance, much to Mary's delight. But all he wanted was her help with his war against France. Mary agreed, with the result that England lost Calais, the last little bit of her once extensive French territory. Fed up, Philip went straight back to Spain and never returned.

Mary said that when she died the words 'Philip' and 'Calais' would be found engraved on her heart. Grieving for the loss of both, she died a year later.

ELIZABETH I - 1558-1603

Meanwhile a skinny, stroppy red-head called Elizabeth was waiting in the wings. Elizabeth had been hanging around on the fringes of royalty all her life. It was a pretty dangerous position, especially if you had some kind of claim to the throne, and were suspected of being ambitious. Elizabeth had already been in and out of the Tower of London, and she was never very far from the shadow of the headsman's axe. She was actually under detention at Hatfield

House when she heard that her half-sister Mary was dead and she was queen.

Always a straight talker, Elizabeth said, 'This is the Lord's doing, and it is marvellous in our eyes!'

Protestants Again

Elizabeth I was crowned at Westminster Abbey in 1558. Almost her first move was to reverse Mary's decision on religion. The bewildered English found themselves officially switched back to being Protestants again. (It's only fair to say that Elizabeth persecuted Catholics almost as much as Mary had Protestants. However, history seems to have forgotten this. Otherwise the cocktail would be called Bloody Lizzy - which might be a bit embarrassing today.)

Elizabeth Rules, OK?

Elizabeth was the last English monarch who really ruled her kingdom. She presided over a golden age in England's fortunes.

Elizabeth encouraged bold sailors (the Spaniards called them pirates) like Drake and Hawkins to roam the seven seas, stealing treasure from Spanish galleons. When Philip of Spain complained, Elizabeth apologised, promised to punish the criminals (if she could find them), and quietly pocketed her share of the loot.

The Virgin Queen

As an unmarried queen Elizabeth was Europe's most desirable bride. There was no shortage of royal suitors. Elizabeth played one against the other, never quite committing herself. In fact she never married, becoming known as 'The Virgin Queen'.

Later historians have questioned her right to this title. She certainly had her royal favourites, handsome and charming aristocrats like the

Earl of Leicester and the Earl of Essex. But Elizabeth was always in charge. It didn't do to get above yourself, or you could really lose your head. Essex, for example, got too ambitious - he was executed for treason in 1601.)

Drama Queen

Elizabeth presided over a splendid court. The arts flourished. In drama particularly there was an explosion of talent. Will Shakespeare was the greatest poet and playwright of the day, and there were many more, men like Ben Jonson, Beaumont and Fletcher, Marlowe and Edmund Spenser of 'Faerie Queen' fame.

THERE WERE A LOT OF POETS AROUND IN
THE TIME OF ELIZABETH I

Queen of Scots

Despite her popularity, Elizabeth had her problems. One of the biggest was a fellow queen, her cousin, the unfortunate Mary Queen of Scots. After a highly-colourful career - which included a stabbed lover and a blown-up husband - Mary was deposed by the straightlaced Scots and fled to England.

This created quite a problem for Elizabeth. Mary was a possible heir to the English throne, and she was a Catholic as well. She was the last person Elizabeth wanted around. But if she sent her back to Scotland she'd be executed.

Elizabeth compromised, keeping Mary in comfortable confinement for eighteen years. Inevitably Mary became a focus for Catholic conspiracies. After all, if something unfortunate happened to Elizabeth, Mary, a Catholic queen, was next in line...

Death Warrant

Elizabeth knew that simply by existing, Mary was a danger to her, but she was reluctant to do anything about it. However, she maintained an excellent spy system. When Sir Frances Walsingham, Elizabeth's James Bond - or rather, her M - produced proof of Mary's involvement in Catholic conspiracies against her, Elizabeth reluctantly signed the death warrant. Mary Queen of Scots was executed at Fotheringay Castle in 1587.

Philip Gets Mad

This upset Catholics everywhere, particularly King Philip of Spain, ex-King Consort of England, who thought he had a right to the English throne himself. He'd originally hoped to get it by marrying Elizabeth, but he'd been forced to realise she was just stringing him along. She had no intention of handing over her kingdom, to him or to anyone else.

When Sir Francis Drake, one of Elizabeth's top sea-captains, added insult to injury by sailing into Cadiz Harbour and burning his ships ('Singeing the King of Spain's beard', Drake called it), Philip decided he'd had enough. In 1588 he prepared a mighty invasion fleet, the so-called Invincible Armada, and set off to conquer England.

The Unlucky Armada

Elizabeth went down to Tilbury to rally the troops. 'I know I have but the body of a weak and feeble woman,' she told them. 'But I have the heart and stomach of a king - and a king of England too.'

The expected invasion never arrived. When the mighty Spanish Armada anchored off Calais, preparing for the attack, Drake's smaller but faster fleet broke up its formation with fireships, then harried the scattered survivors until they fled up the coast of Scotland. There Atlantic gales drove them onto the rocks. Only a few of the ships from Philip's 'Invincible Armada ' made it back to Spain.

Gloriana

The victory was a high point of Elizabeth I's long and successful reign. Hailed as 'Gloriana', she joined in her people's celebration.

Years later in 1601 she told Parliament, 'Though God hath raised me high, yet this I account the glory of any crown that I have reigned with your loves... You never had, nor shall have, any that will love you better.'

It was the simple truth. For all her eager suitors and handsome favourites, Elizabeth I's one true love was England.

Elizabeth I died at Richmond Palace in 1603. She was one of our most loved and most successful monarchs, reigning for an incredible forty-five years.

No wonder that, when our present Queen came to the throne, people looked forward hopefully to a new Elizabethan age...

THE STUARTS

THE STUARTS

When Elizabeth I died unmarried and childless, a strange situation arose. Next in line for the English throne was King James VI of Scotland - son of Mary Queen of Scots, who Elizabeth had executed. In this unlikely fashion the two warring countries were united at last. James I's family name, Stewart, was now spelled Stuart, in the French style, and a new dynasty took over the English throne.

THE PERFECT STUART KING — WARLIKE AND BLOODY

JAMES I - 1603-1625

When he heard the news of Elizabeth's death, James I of Scotland travelled down to London with his wife, Anne of Denmark. He was crowned at Westminster and King James VI of Scotland became James I of England.

England's new Scottish king was something of an oddity, small and clumsy with a tendency to splutter. Conceited and suspicious, with a high opinion of his own abilities, he was known as 'the wisest fool in Christendom', Full of strange opinions and obsessions, he wrote a warning book about witches, and another attacking the evils of tobacco.

Despite his married state, James I had a tendency to form obsessive attachments to handsome young men, and he had a number of 'favourites'. To one of them, George Villiers, whom he created Earl of

JAMES I
HE SUFFERED FROM TERRIBLE NOSEBLEEDS

Buckingham, he wrote, 'God bless you my sweet child and wife... your dear Dad and husband James.' (Say no more...)

Although James I was a Protestant, his mother was a Catholic, and England's still-persecuted Catholics hoped he would make things easier for them. When he failed to do so, a group of Catholic conspirators, organised by Sir Robert Catesby, wanted to protest with a bang. With the help of a Catholic convert called Guy Fawkes they planned to blow up both King James and his Parliament at the state opening in 1605. You can guess the date - November the 5th!

Gunpowder Plot

Renting a house next to Parliament, they dug a tunnel to the House of Lords and filled a cellar with gunpowder. Somebody squealed, a search of the House of Lords was ordered, and Guy Fawkes was discovered with the gunpowder at midnight and arrested - luckily before he had time to strike a match.

Fawkes and his fellow conspirators were executed - and Bonfire Night was born. Guy Fawkes and fireworks have been linked ever since. No-one remembers the conspiracy, but everyone loves the bonfires and the bangs. (Some cynics say Guy Fawkes is the only man who ever went to Parliament with a really practical policy.)

Divine Right

James soon started upsetting his new subjects by talking of 'the divine right of kings'. This meant that the authority of the king came direct from God, and couldn't be questioned by men. The idea wasn't popular with the British and it was to cause at least one future monarch a lot of trouble.

Baronetcies for Sale

James I ruled for long periods without a parliament, relying upon the advice of his courtiers and favourites. Since no parliament meant no money, he raised extra cash by inventing the new rank of baronet, flogging off the honour at £1000 a go.

A Royal Disaster

Always a bit of a glutton, James I developed a severely upset tummy and died in 1625. There were rumours of poison, but a more likely cause was kidney failure, caused by too much food and wine. All in all, James I was a pretty disastrous king. He turned a strong and popular monarchy into a much-weakened institution - soon to be faced by open rebellion...

CHARLES I - 1625-1649

When James I died, his first son, James, was already dead of typhoid. He was succeeded by his second son, Charles.

CHARLES I
HE SHARED THE SAME HAIRSTYLE AS
HIS HORSE (SEE ALSO CHARLES II AND HIS DOG)

A small, slender man, handsome, regal and impressively dignified, Charles I was a much more attractive character than his father. His worst mistake was believing in his dad's daft idea about the divine right of kings. The country had spent hundreds of years training its royal rulers to be reasonable. It had no intention of putting up with a return to tyranny.

Parliamentary Punch-up

The clash with Parliament came almost immediately. When it refused to obey his commands, Charles dissolved it, ruling without a parliament for eleven years. The need for money forced him to summon it again, and when it still proved rebellious, the king sent armed soldiers into Parliament in an attempt to arrest the ringleaders. (They got away.) To this day, no subsequent monarch has ever been allowed to enter Parliament.

Roundheads and Cavaliers

Civil war broke out between the Parliamentarians, or Roundheads (with skinhead haircuts) and the king's party, the Cavaliers (with long flowing ringlets).

There's an old saying - 'The Roundheads were right but repulsive, the Cavaliers wrong but romantic!'

After a series of bloody battles the Royalists were finally and decisively defeated by Oliver Cromwell's New Model Army at the battle of Naseby in 1645.

Charles Surrenders

In 1646 Charles surrendered to the Scots, who promptly handed him over to the English. After a spell of imprisonment, while the Roundheads tried to decide what to do with him, he was put on trial in Westminster Hall before a tribunal of judges.

Even at this late date Charles might have saved his neck by being reasonable. However, he behaved with total arrogance. Insisting on the 'divine right of kings', he refused to admit that any court had the power to try him. To convince him he was wrong, the Roundheads condemned him to death.

Execution

Charles I was executed in Whitehall on 30 January 1649. He wore two shirts. It was a cold day, he said, and if he shivered people might think he was afraid.

The execution of Charles I remains one of the most astonishing events in British history. The whole country was shocked when it actually happened. Even the Roundheads seemed stunned by what they'd done.

One of the judges who'd signed the death warrant wrote, 'One wondered that so good a man should be so bad a king.'

Oliver Cromwell looked sadly at the corpse and muttered, 'Cruel necessity!'

A Second Charles

In 1650, Charles I's son, now Charles II (if you were a royalist, that is) tried a royal come-back. He'd escaped to France after Naseby and returned to Scotland, where he raised an army and was crowned King of Scots at Scone.

A ROYAL ADVISOR HAS A FEW
WORDS WITH THE YOUNG CHARLES II

He marched for Britain, was soundly defeated at the Battle of Worcester, and escaped to the continent - again.

Cromwell's Republic

Britain was declared a republic and Oliver Cromwell became Lord Protector. When Parliament gave him problems he simply dismissed it. For the next nine years Britain had exactly what it had cut off the king's head to avoid - an absolute ruler whose powers couldn't be questioned.

OLIVER CROMWELL'S FAMOUS REQUEST
WHEN HAVING HIS PORTRAIT PAINTED

It was a pretty grim time. Cromwell and his followers were sober, passionately religious men. Theatres and taverns were closed, frivolity and jollity discouraged. The country didn't care for it and the republic, or Commonwealth as it was called, only lasted as long as Cromwell was alive to hold it together.

Charles Comes Home

When he died in 1658 there was a half-hearted attempt to replace him with his son Richard, but the country had had enough of being a dull and sober republican dictatorship. In 1660 the army sent poor Richard packing, and sent off to the continent for the exiled King Charles II, son of the executed - some said martyred - king.

CHARLES II - 1649-1685

We come now to the most romantic of British monarchs. Even Barbara Cartland couldn't have come up with a king like this.

Tall - well over six feet.

Dark - a swarthy complexion, a lady-killer's moustache and long curling black ringlets.

CHARLES II

A LAID-BACK KINDA GUY

Handsome, in a laid-back, devilish way. Incredibly charming as well, with the same warm and friendly manner for everyone, regardless of rank.

They just don't make kings like that any more.

Hard Times for Charles

Witty, relaxed and cynical, Charles II was the first British king for quite a while to have had his share of hard knocks. As a teenager he'd accompanied his father through all the battles and defeats of the Civil War. As a nineteen-year-old king, he'd made a gallant but doomed attempt to regain his throne, only to face defeat once more.

He'd escaped after the battle, crossing a countryside swarming with Roundheads, disguised as a servant, with a price on his head, hiding in an oak tree to escape Roundhead soldiers. He'd been protected by all sorts of ordinary people, who'd risked their lives to save his.

CHARLES II HAS FUN WITH HIS DOG

As an embarrassing and hard-up royal exile, he'd hung around the courts of France and Holland for over ten years, while his supporters schemed to put him back on his throne. When the crown was simply handed back to him without even a fight it must have seemed too good to be true.

Back to Stay

Charles II returned to the throne of Britain with one firm ambition - to stay on it. He was determined never to go on his travels again. He was crowned, for the second time, in 1661.

(The Roundheads had broken up and flogged off all the royal regalia and a new set had to be made - it's still in use today.)

FUNNY HOW SOME DOGS LOOK LIKE THEIR MONARCHS

Charles turned out to be a wise, not to say cunning ruler. If he was a bit of a good-time Charlie, that was what the country wanted after years of sober Puritan rule. The restoration of the monarchy was the signal for a general good time. Ale sales went up, theatres were re-opened and the drama flourished again.

(They even re-discovered sex. Some Restoration plays are such hot stuff they were banned for years, and are only just being performed again today.)

Money, Money, Money

Charles II's biggest problem was lack of money and he tried various cunning methods to improve the royal cash-flow.

In 1662 he married a Portuguese princess, Catherine of Braganza, who brought him a dowry of £300,000 with a couple of naval bases at Tangier and Bombay thrown in. He sold Dunkerque, our very last French possessions back to France for £400,000. He even got a secret subsidy from King Louis IV, promising to restore Catholicism in Britain and to turn Catholic himself.

(The first promise he had no intention of keeping. The second, as we'll see later, he put off till the very last minute.)

Fire and Plague

In the early years of his reign Charles had two major disasters to deal with. In 1665 the Great Plague struck London, killing over 100,000 of its citizens. Charles stayed on in London longer than most, but eventually had to remove the court to Richmond for a time.

In 1666 there was the Great Fire of London. It started in a bakery in Pudding Lane and raged for the next four days until the wind dropped and the fire burned itself out. Charles and his brother James helped the demolition gangs fighting the fire.

(We have vivid descriptions of the Plague, the Great Fire, and of all the main events of Charles II's Court, thanks to the diaries of Samuel Pepys, a civil servant in the Navy Department at the time.)

A New St Paul's

After the fire Christopher Wren, the great architect of the time, supervised the rebuilding of over fifty City churches - including the new St Paul's Cathedral.

Royal Affairs

Despite the fact that he was genuinely very fond of his placid Portuguese wife, Charles II was famous for the number and variety of his mistresses. They ranged from the lowly but lovely orange-seller Nell Gwynne to such proud and aristocratic beauties as Barbara, Lady Castlemaine.

Rival mistresses fought like fury, but Charles, in his lazy way, was affectionate to all of them. His marriage to Catherine turned out to be childless, but Charles more than made up for this with the large number of his illegitimate children.

Illegitimate Dukes

He was good to them as well, seeing that they were well provided for, and elevating quite a few of them to the aristocracy.

Many of today's Dukes - Richmond, Grafton, St Albans and others - owe their noble rank to Charles's paternal generosity.

(It puts today's Charles/Camilla fuss into a totally different perspective when you realise that being a royal mistress is an ancient and honourable profession...)

A Royal Farewell

Charles died in 1685, lingering on for several days after a stroke. (Courteous and considerate as ever, he apologised to the waiting court for being 'an unconscionable time a-dying'.) Keeping his word to King Louis at last, he converted to Catholicism on his deathbed. The Earl of Rochester had already written Charles II's epitaph:

'Here lies our Sovereign Lord the King

Whose word no man relied on

Who never said a foolish thing

Nor ever did a wise one.'

It's a witty but not quite fair summing-up. The most attractive if the most immoral of all our kings, Charles II managed to achieve most of his ambitions. He kept the peace, and he kept his throne.

Perhaps he was best described by one of his contemporaries:

'He was an exact knower of men.'

And women too, of course...

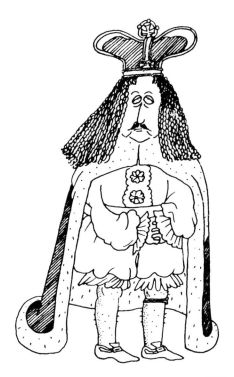

ROYAL PORTRAITS EMPHASIZED THE LENGTH AND ELEGANCE OF THE MEN'S LEGS. IN REALITY, OF COURSE, THEY HAD SHORT, FAT, HAIRY ONES LIKE ANYONE ELSE

JAMES II - 1685-1688

Since Charles II had died without children - legitimate children that is - the throne passed to his younger brother James, who lacked not only his older brother's charm, but his tact as well. (He didn't have Charles's good taste in women either. James's mistresses were all notoriously ugly. Charles used to say he must be doing some kind of penance.)

A Catholic King

A superior, not to say stuck-up character, James became a late convert to Catholicism in 1670, together with his second wife. He came to the throne determined to restore the authority of the monarchy and the supremacy of the Catholic religion. (Charles had inclined towards Catholicism too. Unlike James, however, he had the sense to see that the Catholic-Protestant issue was politically explosive, always steering a middle course to avoid unrest.)

Monmouth's Rebellion

When the new king's intentions became known there was instant rebellion. In 1685 the Duke of Monmouth, eldest of Charles II's ennobled bastards, set himself up as the Protestant champion and claimed the throne. He even had himself crowned at Taunton.

James sent an army against him, and Monmouth was defeated at the battle of Sedgemore. Monmouth was captured and taken to London. He had rebelled before, and the good-natured Charles had always pardoned him. James was far less forgiving, and Monmouth was executed. Judge Jeffries, the notorious 'hanging judge', dealt with the rest of the rebels at Taunton Assizes, hanging many of them, and sending others into slavery in the West Indies.

Catholic Again?

The rebellion would have given anyone less obstinate than James second thoughts, but he pressed on with his plans for restoring

Catholicism. He began by issuing a Declaration of Indulgence, lifting restrictions on anyone not strictly C of E. Seven bishops protested and James slung them into the Tower.

Strangely enough, the last straw was the birth of a son, in 1688, to James's second wife. Britain had been willing to put up with a Catholic king so long as his heirs were Mary and Anne, his two Protestant daughters by his first wife.

But when their Catholic king produced a Catholic heir, it was all too much for Britain, by now a determinedly Protestant country.

PRINCE WILLIAM
OF SATSUMA

WHY WILLIAM OF ORANGE??
WHY NOT ?

HOW ABOUT WILLIAM OF MIXED
FRUIT ?

OR EVEN WILLIAM OF BANANA ?

A Glorious Revolution

James II's nephew William of Orange, the Protestant ruler of Holland, was *invited* by Parliament to invade Britain 'to rescue the nation and the religion'. Not only was William a Protestant, he was married to James II's eldest daughter Mary, which gave him some kind of claim to the throne. As William landed and marched towards London, gathering support on the way, James fled. He took the next boat for France, dropping the sign of his kingship, the great seal of Britain, into the Thames.

It had been a very British revolution.

William III and Mary II - 1689-1702

The Glorious (because bloodless) Revolution of 1688 set a new king and queen on the British throne. They were a bit of an odd couple. William was an ugly hook-nosed little chap, with a habit, like one or two earlier kings, of forming warm friendships with handsome young men. (Oh no, not again!)

His wife Mary, a strapping great woman, towered above him.

Nevertheless, they were a devoted, though childless, pair.

The crowning of William and Mary - they were offered the crown together, in a kind of royal package deal - changed the position of our monarchy forever.

Just look at what had happened.

A New Kind of King

The British people and their Parliament had decided that they didn't want an absolute monarch ruling them by divine right - emphasising their point by cutting off a king's head.

Pretty soon they'd come to the conclusion that they didn't want a republic or a dictatorship either.

Nor did they want a king who would try to turn the clock back - especially if he was Catholic as well.

What they did want was made clear in the Bill of Rights - the package William and Mary agreed to when they accepted the throne.

No Catholic could become king or queen.

No taxes could be raised without parliament's permission.

No laws could be passed without parliamentary approval.

William the Conqueror - remember him? - would have had a fit. The British had rejected their rightful king, *chosen* his replacements - and laid down a new job description as well.

Things would never be the same again.

Battling Billy

Now that he had the throne William had to fight to keep it - but the odd-looking little man was a tough and skilful commander in war. A rebellion in Scotland was swiftly and efficiently suppressed.

The exiled ex-king James attempted to launch a come-back in Ireland. William defeated him at at the Battle of the Boyne. (An event still celebrated by Protestants in Ireland today.)

Mary died of diphtheria in 1694. The heartbroken William said he had never known her to have a single fault.

From then on William had to rule alone.

William at War

In 1701 the exiled James died in France. Just to make things difficult, Louis XIV of France immediately recognised James's son, another James, as King James III of England.

William formed an alliance with Holland and Austria to prevent the thrones of France and Spain from joining up. A complicated struggle known as the War of the Spanish Succession broke out.

The Gentleman in Velvet

In 1702 William, who was a keen horseman, was riding at Hampton Court. His horse stumbled over a mole-hill and the king was thrown, breaking his collar-bone. Pneumonia set in, and William died a few days later.

When the news reached France the exiled Jacobites - supporters of the alternative King James III - raised their glasses in a toast: 'To the little gentleman in velvet...'

ANNE - 1702-1714

On William's death the crown passed to his late wife's sister Anne. She was a kind, rather dim woman, happily married to the even dimmer Prince George of Denmark.

ANNE I
WEARING A DRESS THAT SHE COULD GROW
INTO, AS BRANDY MADE HER RATHER STOUT

('I've tried George drunk and I've tried him sober,' Charles II said despairingly some years earlier. 'There's nothing in him either way!')

The tragedy of Anne's life was her inability to produce healthy children. She had seventeen, all of whom died young.

Parliament and Politics

By this time the foundations of party politics were starting to emerge in Parliament, with Tories, who supported the crown, against Whigs, who favoured the aristocracy.

(The common people still weren't getting much of a look-in.)

Leaving government to her ministers, Anne took little part in politics - though she did once refuse her royal consent to a Parliamentary bill. (She was the last monarch to do this.)

Freeman and Morley

A big feature of Anne's life was her intense friendship with Sarah Churchill, wife of the Duke of Marlborough - the two called each other Mrs Freeman and Mrs Morley.

Anne grew very stout in her later years, due partly to her growing fondness for brandy. When she died in 1702 after a series of strokes she was so fat they had to make a specially-large square coffin for her. (I pity the poor pall-bearers!)

THE HOUSE OF HANOVER

THE HOUSE OF HANOVER

When Queen Anne died without an heir, it wasn't easy finding the next candidate for the crown. The most suitable Protestant candidate - it had to be a Protestant, remember - was George, Elector of Hanover, Germany, eldest son of Charles II's cousin Sophia.

It was a pretty distant connection but it was the best that could be done. The crown of Britain passed to a new dynasty. For some reason they all seemed to be called George...

GEORGE I - 1714-1727

George I was a large, solid Hanoverian who spoke almost no English. Totally German by birth and upbringing, he didn't think very much of his new country and his new subjects.

WINNERS OF A NEW RACE TO THE THRONE

By and large they felt much the same about him. Some of them felt they could do without him altogether.

In 1715 there was a rebellion in Scotland by the Jacobites, as the supporters of the exiled James III were called, but it was soon suppressed.

Britain's German King

The fact that the new king spoke so little English did have one big advantage. Since he never really knew what was going on, George was forced to leave the government of Britain to his ministers. He chose a trusted minister to represent the royal interest in Parliament, and to make sure the vote on the royal salary went through. This favoured official gradually became known as the king's First, or Prime Minister - and a new political post was born.

Too Many Melons

George I was always happiest back in Hanover. While he was away, his British subjects got on perfectly well without him.

On his last trip back to Germany, George was passing through Holland when he unwisely stopped and gorged himself on melons. He was taken ill soon afterwards, and carried on to the nearest town where he died of a cerebral haemorrhage a few days later.

George I was buried in Hanover, close to the tomb of his mother Sophia. Britain's reluctant king was back home at last.

GEORGE II - 1727-1760

Born, and largely brought up, in Hanover, George II was very nearly as German as his father - with whom he'd never got on. He did, however, speak English, though with a heavy accent.

'Dat is vun big lie!' he said, when told his father was dead and he was king at last. He was 44.

A Soldier King

George II was a tall man with bulging blue eyes and a big nose. Better-mannered than his grumpy father, he got on well with his ministers. He enjoyed a prosperous reign, and was the last British king to lead his army in battle, defeating the French at Dettingen in 1743.

In 1745 those persistent Jacobites had another go at regaining the throne. This time they were led by Charles Edward Stuart, grandson of the deposed James II, son of the Old Pretender, the so-called James III.

Bonnie Prince Charlie

The Young Pretender, also known as Bonnie Prince Charlie, was a more attractive and charismatic character than either his dad or grandad. He certainly had the gift of inspiring loyalty. He landed in Scotland with a handful of supporters and soon raised an impressive army from the fierce Highland clans.

The Prince's army met and defeated the English at Prestopans, and the road to England seemed open. But the Prince delayed too long in Scotland, giving the English time to muster their armies.

Butcher Cumberland

George II's brother, the Duke of Cumberland, defeated the rebels in 1746 at the Battle of Culloden. After the battle the Duke of Cumberland hunted down the rebels with such brutal efficiency that he became known as Butcher Cumberland.

Protected and sheltered by his loyal clansmen, and comforted by the famous Flora MacDonald, Bonnie Prince Charlie escaped to France. He died in exile in Rome in 1788. The Jacobite dream was over.

An Empire is Born

As well as rebels at home there were enemies abroad to be dealt with. Thanks to Prime Minister Walpole, the early years of George

II's reign were peaceful. But after 1739 there were long years of war against Spain and France.

In India and North America, British soldiers and administrators fought to gain control of faraway lands.

In 1757 Robert Clive won Bengal for Britain. In 1759 James Wolfe captured Quebec, chasing the French from Canada. Suddenly the British Empire was born - and it grew with amazing speed.

Musical George

The Hanoverians are often accused of a lack of culture. It's perfectly true that George II's main interests were war and history. He didn't think much of art and literature either, saying it was 'All bainters and boets!'

GEORGE II GETS TOTALLY
CARRIED AWAY AT A CONCERT

He did, however, have a great love for music. When he first heard the Hallelujah Chorus in Handel's *Messiah* he leaped to his feet in delight - a tradition that's still followed today.

The British were getting used to their German kings by now. When George II died in 1760, aged 77, he was mourned as a well- loved monarch.

GEORGE III - 1760-1820

Quite a few kings - and queens - live to a good old age and enjoy long reigns. Fine for them, but tough on the prince-in-waiting - who can easily be middle-aged before he gets to plant the royal posterior upon the throne. (Like our own, still-waiting Charlie, with little to do but grumble about modern buildings, go skiing and talk to the trees...)

The case of George III makes you think this long wait may not be such a bad thing. In George's case the crown skipped a generation. George II's eldest son Frederick died before his father, and the crown passed to the king's *grandson* - yet another George. As a result, George III came to the throne when he was just twenty-two, over-flowing with youthful energy and determined to make his mark. The result was disaster.

A British King

It all started off very promisingly. George III was the first of the Hanoverian kings to be born and brought up in England.

He could actually speak English.

He even thought of himself as being British, not German.

'I glory in the name of Briton!' he said.

Tall, handsome, and charming George III looked like being the most popular monarch for years. He was crowned in 1761 and married the same year. The bride was Princess Charlotte of Mecklenburg and the young couple seemed ideally suited. (Well, they must have got on fairly well - they had fifteen children.)

Farmer George

The young king and queen lived pretty simply for royalty. The king was keen on agriculture. He ran model farms at Windsor and Richmond. His subjects nicknamed him 'Farmer George'.

He went walkabout in the streets, chatting affably to his people. So far so good. But Farmer George was young and keen.

He had ideas - never a good thing in a king.

Young George thought that previous monarchs had given away too many of the royal powers. He thought that Parliament was getting above itself, and that the Whigs in particular were having things too much their own way.

He wanted to rule - and we've already seen where that leads.

George III didn't lose his head, not literally. But he may well have lost us America.

The King's Friends

The trouble was, George started to interfere. He even formed his own party, the King's Friends, so that he could by-pass Whigs and Tories and have a direct influence on Parliament.

In 1770 he appointed his own Prime Minister, Lord North. Not the brightest of politicians, North's main qualification was that he never argued with the king, and could usually get Parliament to follow the royal will.

Colonies in Revolt

The American colonies had grown up almost casually, starting out as trading ventures back in the time of Elizabeth I, uniting to fight against the French, growing stronger and more independent year by year. When they first began to rebel, they had a few perfectly reasonable grievances that could easily have been resolved. No-one really wanted to break away from Britain. (George Washington was widely regarded as a dangerous extremist!)

All the colonies wanted was a fairer deal, especially in matters of taxation. North's administration handled the colonists so clumsily that they practically drove them to open rebellion.

In 1776 the enraged Americans signed their Declaration of Independence. The Revolutionary War broke out. Not surprisingly, North's government managed to lose it.

George Gets the Blame

The country was furious, and George III got a lot of the blame. The House of Commons passed an angry resolution.

'The influence of the Crown has increased, is increasing - and ought to diminish!'

For a while poor old George was so unpopular that he seriously considered abdication. He withdrew from active politics and the storm of anti-royal sentiment died down.

Revolution in France

In France, however, the same storm was rising fast. The French had never learned to control their kings at all, and the long-oppressed French people suddenly exploded. The French King Louis was executed. So was his wife, Marie Antoinette, and most of the aristocrats in France. The respectable British were outraged. They'd executed a king themselves of course, but that was well over a hundred years ago!

Before long Britain and France were at war - a war that was to go on, with one or two rest periods, for the next twenty years.

(It's interesting to note that in France, just as in Britain, the republic soon turned into a dictatorship. The French, however, didn't manage to call a halt. First Consul Napoleon became Emperor Napoleon and the French were back where they'd started - with an absolute ruler.

Britain United

In a sense the French Revolution saved the British monarchy. At first the revolutionary spirit seemed as if it might take off in Britain too. But as the British united in the long struggle against Napoleon, the king and his family became symbols of national pride once more.

The Madness of George III

George III had an even more tragic struggle upon his hands. For years he had suffered attacks of an illness called porphyria. Time and again he managed to throw the illness off, but as the years went by the attacks became more frequent and more severe.

The illness produced mania, and by 1810 the king was completely insane. The Prince of Wales was made Prince Regent of the United Kingdom, taking his father's place as head of state.

George III spent the last ten years of his life at Windsor. He gradually became blind and deaf, and for most of the time he was mad. It was a tragic end to a reign that had begun so well.

GEORGE IV

HE MADE INDIGESTION
FASHIONABLE

George IV - 1820-1830

Despite his mistakes, George III had regained the monarchy's popularity, at least until illness struck him down.

George IV, the former Prince Regent, threw the whole thing away. It was all the result of a whole series of long-running scandals, with the kind of ludicrous carrying-on that we haven't seen since - well, since today's tabloids.

True Love

George IV started out as a handsome if rather portly young prince. Vain, spendthrift, and utterly featherbrained, he found the traditional waiting period hard to bear. He ran up huge debts and had a string of mistresses. All that was more or less to be expected - but it was true love that really got him into trouble.

He fell madly in love with a respectable Roman Catholic widow called Maria Fitzherbert. Since he couldn't get her into bed any other way he married her. Well, sort of... According to the Royal Marriage Act, it was illegal for him to marry without his father's permission - which he certainly hadn't got. Rumours about the marriage soon spread all over London, causing a fine old scandal.

Money Troubles

The prince's other main concerns were financial ones. He ran up enormous debts building and furnishing his own establishment, Carlton House. He'd already had £30,000 from Parliament and £50,000 a year from his dad. Now he owed a further £250,000. (The amounts are impressive enough even now but it's almost impossible to imagine what they represent in terms of today's money. We're talking millions - maybe billions!)

A Little Place in Brighton

By promising to cut down, the prince actually managed to con enough money out of the king and Parliament to settle his debts. He celebrated by starting to build a little cottage by the sea. It was a mini-palace called the Brighton Pavilion. Its fantastic towers and turrets are very much in evidence in Brighton today.

A Bride for the Prince

It was decided that the prince might settle down if only he got married. Arrangements were made for him to marry his cousin, Princess Caroline of Brunswick. It was disaster from the very first meeting. Princess Caroline was a plain, rather scruffy girl, apparently none too keen on washing. The prince took one look at her, and said loudly, 'I am not well, pray get me a glass of brandy.' He then left the room.

'Is the prince always like that?' asked Caroline. 'I find him very fat, and nothing like as handsome as his portrait.'

Wedding Night Disaster

It was a bad start, and things soon got worse.

The prince only managed to get through the wedding ceremony by getting plastered. According to Caroline he spent his wedding- night

GEORGE IV

HIS WEDDING NIGHT WAS HOT STUFF

lying drunk in the fireplace. At some point, however, he must have managed to perform his marital duties. Caroline became pregnant, and gave birth to Princess Charlotte nine months later.

Soon after the birth the prince suggested a separation. Caroline cheerfully agreed, giving him custody of their baby daughter. (It was his royal duty to try for a son, but he probably couldn't face going through it again.)

Caroline disappeared to live abroad.

At War with Napoleon

All this time the desperate struggle with Napoleon continued. Anxious to help, the prince offered to take some high rank in the army - just a simple field marshal or something like that.

The army politely declined, preferring to rely on Wellington.

The king succumbed to his final madness, and the prince became Prince Regent in 1811. Four years later, Napoleon was finally defeated at Waterloo.

Since he'd been deprived of his military career, the prince simply invented one. When he was king, he often told his dinner guests how he'd led a heroic cavalry charge at Waterloo. Sometimes he even told the Duke of Wellington...

King at Last

On his father's death in 1820 the prince finally became King George IV. He took immediate steps to stop his wife Caroline from coming to the coronation. He offered her an income of £50,000 a year, as long as she went on living abroad. Caroline refused. She knew her rights - she wanted to be queen.

Caroline Comes Home

Caroline returned to England. Dover Castle gave her a fifty-gun royal salute. The London mob cheered her wildly, preferring her to her husband. (Preferring anyone, actually.)

The new king tried to dissolve the marriage. He alleged that Caroline had been living a scandalous life abroad - which she probably had - and got a Bill of Pains and Penalties introduced to look into her conduct. Caroline had to stand trial in the House of Lords, but Parliament didn't like the idea of doing the king's dirty work. The Bill was passed by such a small majority that the embarassed government withdrew it.

London rejoiced and Queen Caroline attended a public thanksgiving service at St Paul's Cathedral, escorted by the Lord Mayor of London and a hundred and fifty horsemen.

No Crown for Caroline

Her baffled husband organised an elaborate coronation ceremony for himself - giving strict orders that Caroline was on no account to be admitted. When the great day came, Queen Caroline turned up at the Abbey and found every door barred to her.

She went home and sent George a defiant note, demanding to be crowned. Then she went to the theatre. She was taken ill with inflammation of the stomach during the performance. A few days later she was dead.

George Settles Down

The later years of George IV's reign proved rather more peaceful than its stormy beginning. In his old age he suffered greatly from gout. He spent much of his time in Brighton at his beloved pavilion, living quietly with Lady Conygham, his last mistress. He died in 1830. In his will he acknowledged Mrs Fitzherbert, the woman he'd married so long ago, as his wife.

Both as Prince Regent and king, George was one of our most disreputable monarchs, though he wasn't without a certain charm. His reign is a sort of backhanded tribute to the strength of the British monarchy. An institution which survived George IV can probably survive anything...

GEORGE IV AND PRINCESS CAROLINE
PAVE THE WAY FOR CHARLES AND DI

WILLIAM IV - 1830-1837

When William IV was told that he was king, he said he'd go straight back to bed - he'd never slept with a queen before. A bluff, solid character, a complete contrast to the flighty George, William had never expected to become king. He was fifty-five years old.

The Sailor King

The third son of George III, he had been sent to sea as a young Prince. Starting as a midshipman, he had served in the navy for many years, rising, not surprisingly, to Admiral of the Fleet. He lived for twenty years with an actress called Dorothea Bland who bore him ten children. (The eldest was made Earl of Munster.)

Eventually the relationship broke up, and Dorothea went abroad. Late in life William married a young princess called Adelaide. They were a devoted couple, and she was kind to his ten illegitimate children. She made an excellent queen.

The death of the Duke of York, William's older brother, put him next in line for the throne. On the death of George IV the old sailor became king.

Reform Bill

William IV's relatively short reign saw the passage of a number of important reforms. In 1832 the king took an important, if somewhat unwilling part in persuading the House of Lords not to block Earl Grey's Reform Bill.

Despite his high score with Dorothea, William IV failed to produce any *legitimate* children.

Next in line for the throne was his niece, the only child of his younger brother the Duke of Kent. William was devoted to his niece but couldn't bear her mother, whom he accused publicly of keeping his beloved niece and himself apart.

William IV died peacefully in 1837. His beloved niece, a small but determined young woman called Victoria, became queen.

VICTORIA - 1837-1901

None of the first three Georges had been all that impressive and the fourth had been a positive disgrace. Sailor William had been adequate but hardly inspiring.

People were starting to wonder, as they do from time to time, if kings and queens were really necessary...

The monarchy badly needed another superstar, and little Vicky turned up trumps. Her incredibly long reign takes us from the end of the nineteenth century to the beginning of the twentieth.

Victoria's Ministers

Victoria's father had died when she was a baby, and she had had a rather lonely childhood. As a young queen she tended to look for father-figures, finding the first in her first prime minister, Lord Melbourne. Relationships with later Prime Ministers varied considerably.

She never really trusted the flamboyant Lord Palmerston - particularly after he tried to have his wicked way with one of her ladies-in-waiting - in Windsor Castle as well!

She couldn't stand the pompous Gladstone either. 'He speaks to me as if I were a public meeting,' she said.

Late for a meeting, Gladstone tried to apologise with a little joke. 'I have three hands, your majesty. A left hand, a right hand, and a little behind hand.'

'We are not amused,' said Queen Victoria.

Delightful Dizzy

On the other hand, she adored the smooth and charming Disraeli. It's easy to see why.

'Everyone likes flattery,' said Disraeli. 'And when it comes to royalty you should lay it on with a trowel.'

Beloved Albert

In 1840 Victoria married her cousin, Prince Albert of Saxe-Coburg-Gotha. They were blissfully happy. Victoria simply adored Albert. They had nine children, four boys and five girls.

In a Britain increasingly dominated by the middle classes, Victoria and Albert gave the monarchy a much-needed respectability. It was an earlier, more successful version of back to basics - the royals as an ideal family, mother and father and well-behaved children gathered around the Christmas tree.

(Albert introduced the Christmas tree to Britain.)

Victoria in Mourning

When Albert died in 1861, after twenty years of marriage, Victoria was devastated, retiring from public life for many years. People started wondering what was the good of a queen you never even saw. There were mutterings about abdication in favour of her son (sounds familiar!) and talk of a republic. Disraeli heard the alarm bells and convinced the queen to return to public life. Soon she was as popular as ever.

John Brown

In later years her attachment to her Highland servant, a bearded giant called John Brown, caused a considerable amount of concern. He treated her with a rough familiarity, frequently scandalising the Court by addressing her as 'Wumman!' Victoria seemed to enjoy it.

Victoria Regina

Queen Victoria's sixty-four-year reign takes in all the main events of the nineteenth century. The penny post, the Irish potato famine, the Great Exhibition of 1851, the Crimean War, the Indian Mutiny, Darwin's 'Origin of Species', the Salvation Army, the beginning of trade unions, education and votes for (nearly) everybody, the Boer War...

The list is endless, and Victoria presided over it all. Over the long year, she changed from nervously-determined young girl to loving wife and mother, and finally to Kipling's black-clad little old lady, 'The Widow of Windsor'.

She dealt with innumerable governments and ministers, always expressing her opinions, always, in the end, accepting her role as constitutional monarch. She became Empress of India in 1876, ruling the British Empire at its peak. Her life began in the age of stage-coaches, and ended at the beginning of the age of flight. When she died in 1901 an age had come to an end.

EDWARD VII - 1901-1910

Victoria's eldest son, like our own Prince of Wales, spent a long time waiting in the wings. In 1863 he married Princess Alexandra, an icily-cool beauty who was unfortunately rather deaf. Although he did his royal duty - they had six children, three boys and three girls - Bertie, as he was then called, sought his pleasures elsewhere.

Edward the Caresser

His portly figure appeared at smart house parties and fashionable resorts. He loved champagne, good cigars, cards and horse-racing. His friendly ways with the ladies earned him the nickname 'Edward the Caresser'.

Not surprisingly, Queen Victoria didn't care for his playboy way of life. However, the fact that she refused to trust him with any official duties left him with nothing else to do but enjoy himself - which he certainly did!

A Playboy King

When he finally got his turn, Edward made a surprisingly good king. His socialising years stood him in good stead. He loved travel and official occasions and genuinely enjoyed meeting people of all kinds. He pioneered the 'world ambassador' role taken up by later royals.

Edward was particularly useful in encouraging the 'entente cordiale', the much-needed improvement in Britain's relations with her old enemy France. In such a good cause, Edward didn't care *how* many trips to Paris he had to make.

WHEREAS MONARCHS OF OLD WERE CHIEFLY CONCERNED WITH KEEPING DOWN THE PEASANTS, EDWARD VII WAS MORE CONCERNED WITH SHOOTING DOWN THE PHEASANTS .

In fact you might say Edward was a martyr to his duty. Too much good living had weakened his health and he suffered from acute bronchitis. He died peacefully in 1910, just after an enjoyable holiday in Biarritz.

THE HOUSE OF WINDSOR

THE HOUSE OF WINDSOR

George V started off with the family name Saxe-Coburg-Gotha. But the First World War came in the early part of his reign and a wave of anti-German sentiment swept the country. At a time like this, a German name was an embarrassment to a British king. In 1917 he changed the family name to Windsor.

The monarchy entered the twentieth century with little real political power - but royal influence and prestige was still very great...

GEORGE V - 1910-1936

Another second son who didn't expect to inherit the throne, George V, like William IV spent his early days at sea.

The original heir to the throne was his elder brother Edward, a flamboyant dandy who was known as 'Prince Collar and Cuffs' - and was said to frequent male brothels. One can't help feeling that Eddie's death from typhoid was greeted with a certain amount of quiet relief in royal circles. George was a more reliable character altogether.

A Troubled Reign

When George V became king he had a reign that was just crammed with troubles. The worst, of course, was the First World War, that terrible chasm between one age and another. It didn't help that George and the German Kaiser were cousins. Nevertheless, George threw himself into the war effort, visiting the front over four hundred times.

After the war there was civil war in Ireland, the General Strike and the Great Depression.

A Simple King

A short, simple man whose greatest pleasure was his stamp collection, George endured it all, helped by a happy marriage to Princess May of Teck. They had six children, five boys and a girl. Unfortunately George's health was never very robust and in 1928 he suddenly fell ill, suffering from blood poisoning of the lung. His health slowly deteriorated and he died, much mourned, in 1936.

Famous Last Words

There are two very different stories about George V's last words. According to one story, the official one, the dying king raised himself upon his pillows and said feebly, 'How is the Empire?'

In the other version the king was approached by a fussy physician who said, 'Don't worry, your majesty, you'll soon be well enough to enjoy another nice holiday at Bognor...'

Fixing him with a stern glare the dying king said loudly, 'Bugger Bognor!' - and passed away.

I know which one I prefer - and if it isn't true, well, it ought to be...

EDWARD VIII - 1936

As you can see by that single date, it's scandal time again. As Prince of Wales, Edward was a real golden boy. Slender, handsome and golden-haired, he was the nation's favourite. He went to parties, he toured the world, he had discreet and attractive mistresses and everybody loved him.

He was shocked by the poverty he saw in the Depression. 'Something must be done,' he said - and everyone felt that here was a royal with heart.

A Prince in Love

Then he fell in love - with just about the most unsuitable woman in the world - a once-divorced and now remarried American woman called Wallis Simpson, in England with her businessman husband. Not exactly pretty, Wallis was slender, dark, sharp-tongued and smart as a whip. When they first met the Prince asked her if she missed central heating.

'You disappoint me, Sir,' said Wallis. 'Every American woman gets the same question. I'd hoped for something more original from the Prince of Wales!'

Stunned by her charm and her cheek, the rather wimpish prince fell completely under Wallis's spell. She dominated him completely. Very soon he gave his aristocratic English mistresses a ruthless heave-ho. He and Wallis became lovers.

The Scandal Grows

So far so good. Everybody knew, but nobody told. The royals had a tighter grip on the press in those days. Even when the prince became Edward VIII nothing *had* to change. With a little discretion they could have gone on with their affair - even if the king eventually had to marry some suitable princess to provide an heir.

But Edward wasn't discreet, and soon the secret was out. Worse still, he wanted to marry his Wallis - now divorced from her second husband. Even today there's no way a twice-divorced Yank can become Queen of Britain. Back in the thirties it was literally unthinkable.

Abdication

But not to the king. He was offered a morganatic marriage, one where any resulting children have no claim to the throne, but that wasn't good enough. Unless he could have the woman he loved by his side, he would abdicate. He may have thought they would never take him up on it. He had always had everything he wanted. Why couldn't he have Wallis as well?

To be fair, Wallis Simpson knew it would never work. She'd have settled quite happily for royal mistress. It was the king who insisted. If he was bluffing, then the bluff was called. In 1936 Edward VIII signed the Instrument of Abdication. He made a brief broadcast to the nation, and it was all over.

The Wandering Windsors

It was arranged that the ex-king would become the Duke of Windsor. As soon as they were married, Wallis Simpson would become Duchess of Windsor. She would not, however, have the rank of HRH - 'Her Royal Highness' - something which annoyed the duke for the rest of his life.

There were more shocks to come. The duke had assumed that he would remain to advise his younger brother, who had suddenly become king. It was made clear to him that his advice wasn't wanted. In fact *he* wasn't wanted.

The Duke and Duchess left Britain for a life of well-heeled exile. The Duke spent the war as Governor of the Bahamas. Then he and the Duchess resumed their wanderings, looking, as someone said, 'More and more tired, and more and more tanned.'

Meanwhile Britain had a new king, and a new queen.

George VI - 1936-1952

George VI was yet another who never really expected to become king. As was the custom with royal second sons, he had gone into the navy, and had seen active service in the First World War. He was the first member of the royal family to learn to fly.

Ill health had ended his naval career. Shy and stuttering, he had always been completely overshadowed by his talented and popular elder brother. Now big brother was gone and he was on his own. And a few short years after his unexpected coronation there was another world war.

GEORGE VI

THE FIRST MEMBER OF THE ROYAL FAMILY
TO LEARN TO FLY

A Royal Family at War

George VI rose to the challenge magnificently, helped by his wife Elizabeth, and their two young daughters, Elizabeth and Margaret. Even in 1940, when the war seemed almost lost, the royal family refused even to consider leaving England. They went through the Blitz with their people, visiting bomb-damaged streets after the air-raids. When Buckingham Palace was bombed the Queen said, 'Now we can look the East Enders in the face.'

All through the war the royal family, father, mother and two daughters provided an example and an inspiration. Princess Elizabeth joined the Women's Royal Auxiliary Corps and learned to drive army trucks.

Post-war Days

After the war came all the problems of reconstruction. The country had been almost bankrupted by the cost of the war. The new Labour government, elected by a landslide, had bold plans for social change, including nationalisation of vital industries and the creation of a national health service.

For the king the years of peace were not to last long. In 1950 he became ill and underwent a series of operations. He seemed to be making a good recovery, but in 1952 he died peacefully in his sleep after a day's shooting at Sandringham. His queen, of course, is still with us, the incredibly old and much-loved Queen Mum.

Elizabeth II - 1952

In 1947 Princess Elizabeth married Prince Philip, a dispossessed Greek prince, who was created Duke of Edinburgh on their marriage. They have four children, Charles, Anne, Andrew and Edward.

So unexpected was the death of her father that the new Queen had to be summoned back from a safari park in Kenya. She was crowned queen in 1952 amidst a huge wave of popular sympathy. Her husband, as Prince Consort, was the first to do her homage.

The Royal Couple

In the early days there were occasional rumours about the still-dashing Philip, who seemed to be dashing about the world leaving the royal wife and kids at home. There were even stories about involvements with a French singer and an English actress. But none of them really amounted to anything, and they were all mild stuff compared to the tales we hear today.

At first the new royal family could do no wrong. Its image just couldn't have been better.

Beautiful queen, handsome husband, charming children...

When did it all start to go wrong?

Margaret the Rebel

The Queen's younger sister, Princess Margaret, is the first really unconventional royal of our times.

Princess Margaret had her own 'set', a gang of wealthy fun-loving young people. She was often seen at parties and in nightclubs. She was sharp-tongued, sometimes matey, sometimes freezingly royal. She spoke her mind and usually got what she wanted. In the 50s she fell in love with an RAF officer, Group-Captain Townsend. A well-connected handsome war hero, an official of the royal household, he seemed an ideal choice.

A Royal Romance

The romance soon became common knowledge. Foreign papers were full of it - but for a long time not a word appeared in the well-trained British press. At last the story broke, and the country prepared for another royal wedding. But there was a major obstacle. Townsend was divorced, and even though he was the innocent party, the marriage was eventually forbidden. It was a tragic mistake.

Separation - and Marriage

Townsend went into exile abroad, while Princess Margaret hit the party trail harder than ever. Eventually she met a trendy photographer, Tony Armstrong-Jones. He wasn't really what you'd call royal material, but at least he wasn't divorced. This time the necessary royal permission was given. In 1960 they were married, with surprisingly little opposition. Armstrong-Jones was upgraded to Earl of Snowdon.

Separate Lives

As time went on, it became clear that the marriage wasn't working out. The royal couple began quarrelling, often in public. Gradually their lives moved apart. Princess Margaret's name became linked with a smooth socialite called Roddy Llewellyn. They were photographed on an island hideaway in the West Indies. A scandal broke and Snowdon asked for a divorce - the first divorce at the heart of the royal family since the days of Henry VIII.

One royal marriage down.

Royals on TV

In 1969 the Queen allowed the BBC to make 'Royal Family', a documentary about the 'private lives' of the Windsors. We saw the

THE QUEEN AND HER QUIET AND FRIENDLY
FAMILY (OF CORGIS)

Queen and her family doing everyday things like having tea and walking the dog. Nothing in the least controversial, of course. The cameramen and commentator were so reverent they must have been working on their knees. Everyone was fascinated - too fascinated perhaps. The public wanted more.

The idea of the documentary was worthy enough, to make the royals more human, more modern and accessible. All the same, it was a first hesitant step towards show-business - an innocent pilot for that steamy royal soap-opera the Queen now wants so desperately to close down.

Anne and Mark

Princess Anne, the Queen's daughter, is a keen horsewoman and another royal rebel. For a long time she had a reputation for being sharp-tongued and stand-offish. She resented the intrusions of the press and was known to tell over-keen cameramen to 'Naff off!' (In later years there has been a very successful attempt to soften her image by emphasising her charity work.)

In 1973 Princess Anne married Captain Mark Phillips. He was an army officer affectionately known to his friends as 'Foggy' and 'Mud' - because he was thick and wet!

Anne and Mark were both keen riders, so at least they had horses in common. In the end it wasn't enough. Over the years the old separate lives syndrome set in.

More Scandal

There were scandals here too. Anne's former bodyguard tried to sell the press allegations about their 'special relationship.'

Then an Australian girl filed a paternity suit against Mark Phillips. (She said he'd invited her to his hotel, leaving his riding-boots outside the bedroom door so she could find the room!) In April 1992 it was announced that Princess Anne was filing for divorce.

Two down.

Randy Andy

The Queen's middle son, Andrew, grew up to be a dashing young naval officer, who saw active service in the Falklands. No intellectual giant, definitely one of the lads - and hell-on-wheels with the ladies. Known, inevitably, as Randy Andy.

A loud-mouthed hearty with a fondness for practical jokes, Andy sprayed paint over the press on a visit to California in 1984. The exploit earned him a new title - 'The Duke of Yob'.

In 1986 he married a big, bouncy redhead called Sarah Ferguson - who'd already been more than just good friends with a well-known racing driver.

For a time things went well. But Andy was away at sea much of the time. When he was home he often abandoned his wife in favour of a day on the golf course.

Favourite Fergie

For a while the colourful Fergie was favourite with the press. But her her love of high life and holidays - especially when she left her

ROYAL NON-BESTSELLERS

new baby at home on a long trip to Australia - came in for criticism. In fact she seemed to be obsessed by holidays, taking seven or eight nearly every year. She was very keen on free gifts and freebies of every kind. She didn't seem to be doing much in the way of public duties either. The fickle press began turning against her, and voted her the 'Worst-value Royal'.

In 1989 Fergie launched on a literary career with a children's book called 'Budgie the Helicopter', saying the profits would go to sick children. It later emerged that only ten per cent of the profits, reckoned at over £100,000, would go to charity.

There was more trouble when Fergie's book was found to be suspiciously close to another story called 'Hector the Helicopter' published in 1961. ('Pure coincidence', said her publishers.)

And now there's talk of a very well paid television deal!

Fergie out of Favour

Then some photographs were found showing her on holiday in Morocco with a Texan millionaire. Everyone said she'd definitely gone too far. But that was nothing to what was to come.

In 1992 Fergie and her financial adviser were photographed on holiday on the French Riviera. The sight of a topless Fergie having her toe sucked caused a world-wide scandal. Andy had had enough. In March 1992 a formal separation was announced.

Three down.

Theatrical Edward

What about Edward, the youngest son? Slender and charming, he had a promising career at school and university, and announced his intention of joining the Royal Marines. It caused quite a fuss when he left the Royal Marines before the end of his training course to work in show business. So far he has worked in the theatre and for a TV production company. His main television achievement so far has been his part in organising a televised 'It's a Knockout' tournament held at Alton Towers in which Fergie - who else - appeared with other young royals, and royal dignity took another knock.

At least there are no problems about young Edward's marriage - people seem to doubt if there's ever going to be one. However, a royal romance has suddenly sprung up - though no-one's setting a date yet.

The Chuck and Di Show

We've been saving the big one till last.

Charles and Diana - Chuck and Di as our American friends say. What a story!

Married in 1981 to *huge* public interest all round the world.

A reasonably handsome prince, a stunning fairytale princess. True, he's twelve years older, a mildly eccentric intellectual, and she's a raving Sloane Ranger with no O levels, but this is Romance, right? Let's not quibble!

In due course the royal couple produce two handsome children, both boys. Harry and William, the traditional heir and spare. The Windsors are set up well into the next century.

Or are they?

BLOODSPORTS HAVE ALWAYS BEEN POPULAR WITH THE MONARCHY

Rumours

By now Diana is an amazingly popular, much-photographed media superstar leaving the scholarly Charles way behind in the public popularity stakes.

Slowly but surely rumours of estrangement start. Every shade of expression is studied when they appear together.

Gradually they stop appearing together.

Diana throws herself into an active social life and is seen with various young men-about-town.

Press stories accuse Charles of being cold and unsympathetic - and of keeping up the old royal mistress tradition after his marriage to the fairytale princess.

A blue-nose bishop says he's not fit to be king.

A tell-all book about Diana comes out, allegedly with her co-operation. We hear about depression, about eating disorders, about suicide attempts...

Royals on Tape

Then come the tapes - mysterious transcriptions of mobile- phone conversations, allegedly picked up and recorded by ham radio operators. Some say this just isn't possible, and that the recordings must have been made from bugged telephones. Bugged by whom?

Leaked by whom - and why? No-one seems to know for sure - but whatever their origins, the tapes are sensational!

Charles in the Camillagate tapes, allegedly talking to his mistress - and saying things you'd blush to remember in private, let alone have recorded and broadcast to the nation.

Diana in the Squidgygate version - Squidgy being some kind of nickname - apparently talking to what sounds very like a lover, whining on about her hard life and all her problems and how unhappy she is.

Incredible! Enough already! In fact - too much!

No wonder the Queen called last year her *annus horribilis*.

What's Gone Wrong With Our Royals?

So what went wrong?

And what, if anything, can be done about it?

Some of it's our fault.

We want the royal family to be noble, remote, impressive. But we also want to know every single thing they say or do - especially the scandalous bits.

We can't have it both ways - and neither can they.

Because it's the royals' fault too. Some of them have been colluding with the situation, positively seeking publicity. They're always on the telly or in the papers and magazines, telling us far too much about themselves.

The Royal Job

As long as the royals do their job, their private lives are their own affair. And what is their job, you ask?

You just have to look at history to realise that what suits Britain best is a constitutional monarchy. Somebody's got to wave from the balcony, and appear on state occasions. The monarchy provides a harmless focus for public ceremony and national sentiment - while the real governing is done by Parliament. If it works - and it does - don't fix it!

We've been centuries getting the right relationship with our royals - and it's a shame to waste all that effort...

THE ROYAL DOG-BASKET

INDEX

A poem to remember them by:

Willy, Willy, Harry, Ste,
Harry, Dick, John, Harry three,
One, two, three Neds, Richard two,
Henry four, five, six then who?
Edward the Fourth and Dick the Bad,
Henry twice and Ned the Lad,
Mary, Bessy, James the Vain,
Charlie, Charlie, James again,
William and Mary, Anna Gloria
Then four Georges, William and Victoria,
Edward the Seventh and George the Fifth,
Edward the Eighth and George the Sixth.

... And Elizabeth

Anon

GLOOM, DOOM AND VERY FUNNY MONEY:
Economics for Half-wits
by Neil Innes

'This is an informative and entertaining guide to the world of economics. If you're still a half-wit after reading this book, you've clearly got a good future working in the City.'
  Neil MacKinnon, Chief Economist, Citibank

A SUSPICIOUSLY SIMPLE HISTORY OF SCIENCE AND INVENTION: Without the Boring Bits
by John Farman

'I found it to be one of the most readable, amusing and informative science books that has come my way for some time... Most highly recommended for anyone who want to put some humour into teaching...'
  Education Review - NUT